WRITERS' HOUSES

Bateman's at Burwash in Sussex, the home of Rudyard Kipling.

WRITERS' HOUSES

a literary journey in England

by MICHAEL and MOLLIE HARDWICK

PHOTOGRAPHY BY MICHAEL HARDWICK

Phoenix House

London

© Text and photographs, Michael and Mollie Hardwick, 1968
© Map, J. M. Dent & Sons Ltd, 1968
All rights reserved
Made in Great Britain
at the Aldine Press, Letchworth, Herts
for J. M. DENT & SONS LTD
Aldine House, Bedford Street, London
First published 1968

Other books by Michael and Mollie Hardwick include

ALFRED DELLER: A SINGULARITY OF VOICE
  Cassell
THE CHARLES DICKENS COMPANION
THE SHERLOCK HOLMES COMPANION
THE MAN WHO WAS SHERLOCK HOLMES
FOUR SHERLOCK HOLMES PLAYS
SHERLOCK HOLMES INVESTIGATES
  John Murray

CONTENTS

The dates are the years in which the writers were associated with their houses.
Each chapter is illustrated by one or two photographs.

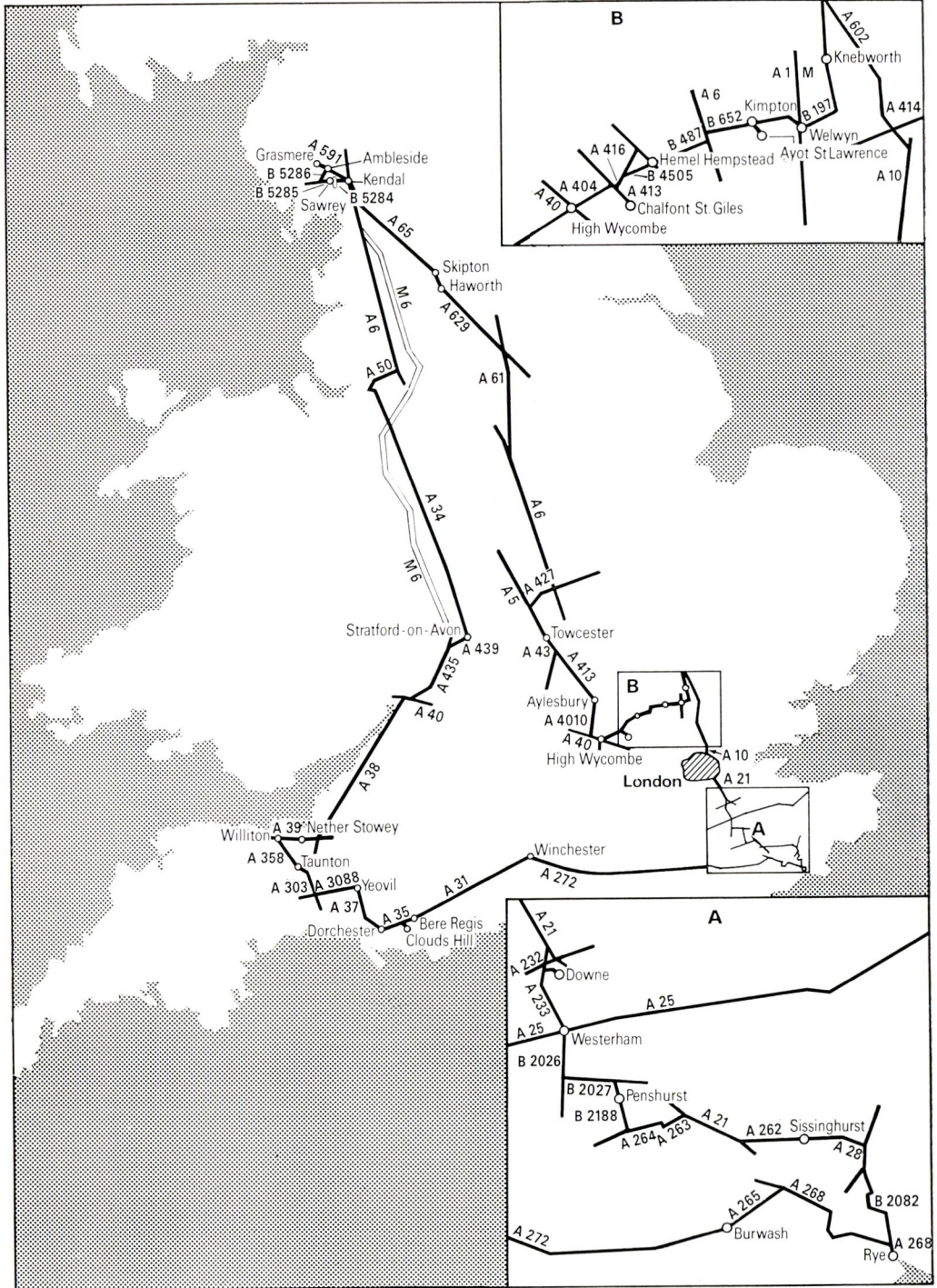

B

A 602
Knebworth
A 1 M
A 6
Kimpton
B 652
B 197
Welwyn
A 414
B 487
Hemel Hempstead
Ayot St Lawrence
A 416
B 4505
A 413
A 10
A 40
A 404
Chalfont St. Giles
High Wycombe

Grasmere
A 591
Ambleside
B 5286
Kendal
B 5285
Sawrey
B 5284
A 65
Skipton
Haworth
M 6
A 629
A 6
A 61
A 50
A 34
A 6
M 6
A 5
A 427
Stratford-on-Avon
A 439
Towcester
A 435
A 43
A 413
A 40
Aylesbury
B
A 4010
A 38
High Wycombe
A 40
London
A 10
A 21
A
Williton
A 39 Nether Stowey
A 358
Taunton
Winchester
A 303
A 3088
Yeovil
A 31
A 272
A 37
A 35
Bere Regis
Dorchester
Clouds Hill

A

A 21
A 232
Downe
A 25
A 233
A 25
Westerham
B 2026
B 2027
Penshurst
B 2188
A 21
A 262
Sissinghurst
A 264
A 263
A 28
B 2082
A 265
A 268
A 268
A 272
Burwash
Rye

PREFACE AND ACKNOWLEDGMENTS

OF ALL the houses of famous people which the general public may visit, those of writers seem to us to stand in a class of their own. While we may admire with awe a nobleman's ancestral pile, most of us do not carry away from it much more than a sketchy knowledge of a being and a way of life far removed from our own; together perhaps with a slightly heightened appreciation of history, architecture and good taste.

With authors and poets we are on more familiar ground. Whether we have read their works, or enjoyed adaptations of them in broadcasting or the theatre or cinema, or merely plodded through them at school, there are points of recognition to make us feel that we are visiting the home of someone we have known, however slightly. If we find that we are amidst the surroundings which saw the birth of a favourite work, we are moved: should it be that we are standing, too, in the very setting of that invention, we know delight.

We thought it would be a pleasant notion to visit most of the writers' houses which are open to the public in England in order to discover something of what they meant to their eminent owners, in terms of the work they did and the lives they lived in them, and to try to convey some impressions that might transcend the guide-book. In doing so, we learned much that we had ignored or forgotten, and found ourselves reading with pleasure books by and about the writers which we might otherwise never have picked up. Even our attitude towards those of them who had always seemed unsympathetic in their ideas or lacking in personal attraction mellowed when we shared briefly what remains of the intimacy of their homes and inspected the little personalia which reminded us that they were, even the most celebrated of them, fellow human beings, not the demi-gods fame has made them seem. The first title to suggest itself for this book was 'An English Literary Pilgrimage'—and we rejected it out of hand.

This was no purely cerebral jaunt. It took us to some lovely parts of England and to a number of houses which we found inviting in their own right. They appeared, with exceptions, to fall into four types: the ancestral and baronial of the born aristocrats like Philip Sidney and Bulwer Lytton; the medium-sized country houses 'of character', as the estate agents would say, tracked down and cherished by such seekers after rural peace and quiet as Kipling, Henry James, Shaw, Darwin and Winston Churchill; the London homes of the urbanites, Johnson, Dickens and Carlyle; and the remote, modest cottages of the poets and the one mystic, T. E. Lawrence. We do not suggest that this grouping proves anything: but it was interesting to try to find out in individual cases why the house and locality had been chosen. With two passing exceptions we have not included birthplaces: we wanted houses in which people had lived of their own volition.

Certain impressions grew with every house we visited. One was the extraordinary 'presence' left in a house by its dwellers, leaving aside subjective fancy or associative ideas. Hughenden is as witty and good-natured as its Dizzy and his Mary Anne; Knebworth as romantically melancholy as Bulwer. We would have given a lot for the corresponding 'feel' of Lamb and Shelley and 'Lewis Carroll'.

Another reflection, and a sad one, is upon the deteriorating effect of time on the human countenance. In many of the houses we visited, portraits of the celebrated occupant at various stages of life were on show, a sequence one never sees in the ordinary home. Each of these impressed heavily upon us the contrast between unclouded, idealistic youth and sickly, disillusioned—even though famous—age.

The other thing that struck us was the inevitable presence of Shaw and Bulwer in the lives of their contemporaries, and of Keats in everyone's.

Any literary-minded car driver with a week to ten days to spare could make an itinerary out of this collection of houses for a pleasant circular tour that would take him to several refreshingly different regions and, except for passing through, no cities after London. Starting with the London houses, he would then drive into Kent, then Sussex, then along the coast across Hampshire into Dorset; up to Somerset, on to the Lake District and Yorkshire; thence back to London, to finish off with a few houses lying near by. This is the order in which we have presented our chapters: the entire journeying amounts to little more than a thousand miles of easily spaced divisions.

We do not claim to have included every house of this kind in England. A few more are in private hands, and though they may be opened for inspection periodically, or to special applicants, their owners are understandably reluctant to draw too much attention to them. One house, Jane Austen's, at Chawton, Hampshire, we exclude with regret because we could not obtain the special permission to take photographs which was so readily granted in every other case. William Morris's house at Kelmscott would have gone in, but was undergoing extensive renovation and was without its contents while the book was being prepared. Other omissions must be ascribed to limitations to this volume's size, or, quite simply, to our ignorance that the places have been preserved for the public to view.

PREFACE AND ACKNOWLEDGMENTS

If this book should move a few of its readers to visit some of these houses, and to find as a result new or renewed enjoyment in their former owners' writings, then its purpose will have been achieved.

We are grateful to the following for their assistance with this book:

KEATS HOUSE: London Borough of Camden, Mr A. Lee, Mrs C. M. Gee.

CARLYLE'S HOUSE: National Trust, Mrs Thea Holme, Mrs M. G. Boucher.

DICKENS HOUSE: The Dickens Fellowship, Miss D. L. Minards.

DR JOHNSON'S HOUSE: Dr Johnson's House Trust, Miss Margaret Eliot.

DOWN HOUSE: Royal College of Surgeons, Mr S. Robinson.

PENSHURST: Viscount De L'Isle, V.C.

CHARTWELL: National Trust, Miss Grace Hamblin, O.B.E.

SISSINGHURST CASTLE: National Trust, Mr Nigel Nicolson.

LAMB HOUSE: National Trust, Mr H. Montgomery Hyde.

BATEMAN'S: National Trust, Mr and Mrs Bruce Sutherland.

CLOUDS HILL: National Trust, Mrs P. Knowles.

COLERIDGE COTTAGE: National Trust, Mrs Eileen M. Dinham.

STRATFORD-ON-AVON: Shakespeare Birthplace Trust, Mr Levi Fox, O.B.E., Miss Shirley Watkins, Mr W. Harry Dyke, Miss H. Sheward.

HAWORTH PARSONAGE: The Brontë Society, Mrs Joanna Hutton.

DOVE COTTAGE: Dove Cottage Trust, Mr L. V. Rickman, Mr and Mrs E. Eastwood.

HILL TOP: National Trust, Mrs Freda Jackson.

HUGHENDEN: National Trust, Mr T. A. Jefferson.

MILTON'S COTTAGE: Milton's Cottage Trust, Mr and Mrs K. C. Meiklejohn.

KNEBWORTH: Lord and Lady Cobbold.

SHAW'S CORNER: National Trust, Mr and Mrs Hugh Broadbridge.

Mr Romilly Fedden of the National Trust.

Permission to quote from the following published works is acknowledged gratefully:

Rudyard Kipling's *Something of Myself*: Mrs George Bambridge and Macmillan & Co. Ltd.

The Letters of T. E. Lawrence, edited by David Garnett: the Executors of the T. E. Lawrence Estate, the editor and Jonathan Cape Ltd.

MICHAEL AND MOLLIE HARDWICK
Great Mongeham, Kent

Keats House was originally two dwellings, in one of which the poet spent his last three years of life. He composed some of his greatest poetry here and fell in love with a daughter of the family next door, Fanny Brawne.

KEATS HOUSE

Hampstead

JOHN KEATS 1818–1820

'IN THE SPRING of 1819 a nightingale had built her nest near my house. Keats felt a tranquil and continual joy in her song; and one morning he took his chair from the breakfast-table to the grass-plot under a plum-tree, where he sat for two or three hours. When he came into the house, I perceived he had some scraps of paper in his hand, and these he was quietly thrusting behind the books.'

The nightingales have flown from Hampstead, the plum tree has perished, but the house where John Keats lived with his friend Charles Brown, where he wrote, on such scraps of paper, some of his greatest poetry, and was most happy and most unhappy, stands today. Hampstead was a country village then, though conveniently near to London. Building, time and communications have urbanized it; but, by some touch of Keatsian enchantment, to pass through the garden gate of Wentworth Place, now called Keats House, is to enter a piece of that rural Hampstead of long ago.

The graceful, compact white house, which began as two houses, was built in 1815 by Charles Armitage Brown, a retired business-man turned author, and his friend Charles Wentworth Dilke. Dilke and his wife and small son inhabited the larger of the semi-detached pair; Brown, a bachelor, the smaller one. They were drawn to the district not only for its pleasant situation, but because 'dear Hampstead, revelling in varieties' was the home of Leigh Hunt and a centre of literary and artistic life. It was probably through Hunt, in 1817, that Brown met John Keats, the young poet whose genius was already acknowledged by men of vision, and 'in that interview of a minute inwardly desired his acquaintanceship, if not his friendship'.

Keats was then lodging in Hampstead. He went often to Wentworth Place to enjoy the company of the genial, down-to-earth Brown, to talk poetry and write it, to eat, and drink his favourite claret in Brown's parlour. In 1818 the two went on a Scottish walking tour. Not long after they returned, Keats moved to Wentworth Place altogether, after the tragically early death, from consumption, of his young brother Tom.

As one crosses the garden of Wentworth Place today, Keats's 'grass-plot' is as green and well kept as ever. The ancient mulberry tree that he knew still drops its fruit on the grass. He and Brown did not use the handsome front door: their entrance was round the side, no longer now giving on to the garden but into the Chester Room, an extension built on by Eliza Chester, a retired actress who bought Wentworth Place in 1838, converted it into one house and added this handsome drawing-room.

The visitor today, using the main front door, enters what was originally the Dilke family's home. To the right of the hallway is their double drawing-room, graceful and essentially unchanged. Here is the pretty fire-grate at which muffins were toasted for Keats's tea, for Maria Dilke took a motherly interest in the young man. 'Mrs Dilke is knocking at the wall for Tea is ready,' he writes to his brother George in America. 'Yesterday when the tray came up Mrs Dilke and I had a battle with celery stalks.'

In this room is a fine Hepplewhite table which belonged to Leigh Hunt. Keats must have sat at it. On the wall is a painting by Keats's friend Joseph Severn of the poet beneath the trees by the Spaniards Inn at Hampstead, listening to a nightingale silhouetted against the moon: sentimental, like most of Severn's paintings of his idolized friend, but irresistibly evocative.

In a showcase in this room are some of the most poignant relics in the house: a portrait and some personal possessions of Fanny Brawne. During the Scottish tour Brown had lent his part of the house to a Mrs Brawne, a widow, and her two daughters and young son. Later, when the Dilkes moved to London, the Brawnes took over their half of Wentworth Place. It had been love at first sight when Keats had been introduced to the eighteen-year-old Fanny Brawne—tiny, beautiful, witty, fashionable, but sensible beyond her years. She was his first and only love. On Christmas Day 1818 they became secretly engaged.

Less than three years later he was dead, aged twenty-five. Fanny's miniature portrait shows a face sadly changed after twelve years without him. Her eyeglasses, also among these relics, are a pathetic reminder of the old age which she attained and he did not. The almandine engagement ring he gave her lies beside the brooch made like a broken lyre, its strings Keats's hair, which she wore until her death.

Passing through where once a wall separated the two dwellings one stands in the hallway of the Keats-Brown house. The Keats sitting-room, looking towards the back garden, is an authentic, restored replica of the room as he knew it and as Severn recorded it in his painting 'Keats at Wentworth Place', which hangs over the fireplace. The shutters Keats fastened are still in place. The carpet has been woven to the design of that shown in the picture. Copies of the chairs over which Keats would drape himself 'like a picture of somebody reading' have been arranged beside the french windows, as if ready for him to sit there again, book in hand, sometimes raising his head to watch the sparrows pecking about the gravel, as he loved to do. A portrait of his idol, Shakespeare, hangs where it used to hang, near

2

On such a 'sopha-bed' in this room in Keats House the poet lay after becoming stricken with consumption, hoping to glimpse his forbidden Fanny Brawne walking in the garden.

the bookshelf where he hid the scraps of paper on which he had just written the *Ode to a Nightingale*. The tiny room is still electric with his presence; not so much haunted as eternally possessed.

Across the hall is the larger sitting-room, which was Brown's. They used it as a communal living-room, and it too has been well restored to the likeness of the room Keats knew. In front of the window stands a 'sopha-bed' of the period, such as the one on which he lay when the tuberculosis that was to kill him had struck him down. 'How much more comfortable than a dull room upstairs, where one gets tired of the pattern of the bed-curtains!' From here he could watch life going past: gipsies on the Heath, a pot-boy with someone's lunch beer, labourers at work on the new houses, two old ladies with a lap-dog. Most eagerly of all he watched for Fanny, walking in the garden in hope of a glimpse of him. She was forbidden to visit him much, for fear of over-exciting him.

In the corner stands a grandfather clock which left the house with Brown in 1822 and has now returned from New Zealand where he died. On the wall are copies of grotesque heads from Hogarth's 'Rake's Progress', made by Brown; and on another wall a copy of Hogarth's 'Sleeping Congregation', which gave Keats 'a psalm-singing nightmare'. While he was still in health he wrote in this room some of his richest poetry during his golden year of 1819; and, in his last spring, many brave, infinitely sad notes to Fanny. 'All we have to do is to be patient . . . I am kept from food so feel rather weak—otherwise very well . . . illness is a long lane, but I see you at the end of it . . . send me the words Good Night to put under my pillow.'

It was in his bedroom, enlarged since his day by the taking-in of a passage, that he first coughed the ominous spot of arterial blood which he knew to be his death-warrant. The room is almost unfurnished, but the bell-pull is still there which he must often have used to summon the devoted Brown, his nurse for many weeks during the winter of 1820. Over the fireplace hangs a copy of the last drawing made of him by Severn, as he lay on his death-bed in Rome in January 1821. With the cruelty of ignorance the doctors had banished him there, away from Hampstead and his friends, in terrible exile from Fanny. Downstairs, in a case in the Chester Room, is the last letter he wrote from Italy to Mrs Brawne. To Fanny he could bear only to add a postscript: 'Good bye Fanny! God bless you.'

The Chester Room is lined with cases housing other important letters of Keats and his circle. Many personal relics include his precious annotated volumes of Shakespeare, Chaucer and Milton, priceless clues to his mind and poetry. A lecture notebook from his days as a medical student contains languidly scribbled anatomical details jostled by delicate little drawings of flowers. The life-mask made of him by his friend Haydon gives a clear impression of the beautiful, virile face, while locks of his red-gold hair, lying near by, have scarcely faded.

The extraordinary affection which Keats inspired in his lifetime in those who knew him ('I am certain', Fanny Brawne said, 'that he has some spell that attaches them

4

to him') has outlasted him. Wentworth Place was rescued from destruction by public subscription when so many other houses of the period perished. When it was damaged in the last war the Pilgrim Trust and the Keats-Shelley Association of America, Inc., were largely instrumental in restoring it. Those who care for it now, and maintain the Keats Memorial Library next door, have brought the house back as near as can be to the state it was in when Keats lived there, even to the detail of stripping the many layers of wallpaper and having copies made of the bottom layers which Keats knew.

It seems a house in which life has been suspended, energy interrupted. There is an air of unfinished business. One hesitates to leave. Then the front door closes, and one crosses again

> *. . . a lawn besprinkled o'er*
> *With flowers, and stirring shades, and baffled beams.*

In a tree, his favourite bird, the thrush, still sings

> *O fret not after knowledge! I have none,*
> *And yet the Evening listens.*

Of all houses, it is the one in which one could wish for a time machine; so that, returning to the year 1819, it might be possible to arrest tragedy with today's medical knowledge. But the gate closes: the hedge of laurustinus and china roses has gone: and we are back in Hampstead, NW3.

CARLYLE'S HOUSE

Chelsea

THOMAS CARLYLE 1834–1881

ONCE, Cheyne Row was orchard land, a pleasant neighbour of Shrewsbury House, one of the stately residences of Tudor Chelsea. The riverside village grew, and in 1708 were built the graceful red-brick houses that form Cheyne Row today. But between their building and 1834, when the Carlyles moved into No. 5, pretty, rural Chelsea had declined socially. 'Chelsea is unfashionable,' wrote Carlyle to Jane in Scotland. 'It was once the resort of the Court and great, however; hence numerous old houses in it, at once cheap and excellent.'

How the sage would stare if he could see Chelsea today, and study the local estate agents' advertisements! With what fanatic violence would he barricade himself into his Silent Room at the top of the house. Cheyne Row itself, however, is a peaceful thoroughfare still, leafy and pleasant, away from the Embankment traffic. The trees that were there when the Carlyles arrived were cut down soon after, but others have grown. The number on the handsome front door is changed—it is now No. 24—but otherwise Jane and Thomas would find its outward semblance very little different.

They took it on a year's lease, and lived in it for the rest of their lives: Jane died in 1866, Thomas in 1881. It saw their early poverty, when £2 10s. 0d. was far too much for Jane to pay for a much-needed sofa; it witnessed the happiest time of her not very happy life, when all her home-making instincts, energy and practical good sense went into creating this home for Thomas, her beloved, difficult husband. In 1834 he was unknown, *Sartor Resartus* not yet published, the *History of the French Revolution* only a plan for the future. He had renounced Christianity but declared war on atheism; he was at the start of his career as a philosophical radical giant among historians, and stern adviser to a fault-ridden world. Jane knew that he was going to be an important man. Gladly she agreed to leave Scotland and become a Londoner, if it would be best for Thomas. They arrived at Cheyne Row in high spirits. On the way, Jane's canary, Chico, had burst out singing. They took it for a good omen.

There are canaries in the dining-room window today. An agreeable room, Thomas considered this, when it had been made bright and comfortable by Jane during those

6

Thomas Carlyle converted an attic into this Silent Room in order to escape the noise of his Chelsea neighbours and their fowls; but his wife Jane called it the noisiest room in the house.

cheerful 'Gypsy days' of settling in: an old carpet from their Scots home nailed down by her own delicate hands, and patched up with bits of others; her table and little piano in position. Over the mantelpiece hangs Robert Tait's picture 'A Chelsea Interior'. It is like a reflection of the room and of the Carlyles of 1857: a haggard, bearded man and a sick woman, very different from the handsome young Thomas of Lawrence's drawing, and the deliciously pretty Jane, swan-necked, large-eyed, and bright-ringleted, of the loveliest miniature of her. Looking at Jane as one meets her in portrait after portrait, it seems astonishing that although her contemporaries called her many good things, they never called her a beauty. It was in this room that the gallant and impressionable Leigh Hunt, their neighbour, was warmly greeted by Jane one day, and celebrated it in verse:

> *Jenny kissed me when we met,*
>   *Jumping from the chair she sat in;*
> *Time, you Thief, who love to get*
>   *Sweets into your list, put that in!*
> *Say I'm weary, say I'm sad,*
>   *Say that health and wealth have missed me,*
> *Say I'm growing old—but add*
>   *Jenny kissed me!*

Weary, sad and old they all grew, but the kiss was immortal: and the very 'chair she sat in' is still in this room full of things they knew and touched.

The broad staircase 'with massive balustrade (in the old style),' as Thomas described it to Jane, leads to the first floor. The Carlyles were certainly not antiquarians, for in their great renovations of 1852 they had the pine panelling of the hall and staircase covered by wallpaper, and painted and grained to resemble wood. That the house preserves most of its ancient, mellow character today is certainly not due to Thomas and Jane. One feels that had their finances been up to it they would have modernized it briskly from attic to cellar. The first-floor library or drawing-room (it was used as both because of shortage of space) was enlarged, the panelling and 'queer old presses' flanking the fireplace removed, the fireplace rebuilt, the windows altered. The result is a largish Victorian room with no character of its own, only that of Thomas and Jane. Part of his library and much Carlyleana are here, including the thirty-two volumes of Goethe's works presented by Goethe, whom Carlyle revered as a god. The famous sofa is here, Jane's 1835 bargain, a luxury after the hard furniture they had had to put up with. 'Oh, it is so soft! so easy!' In 1849 Jane had written: 'I have been busy, off and on, for a great many months, in pasting a screen . . . all over with prints. It will be a charming "work of art" when finished.' It is such a charming work of art that one lingers by it, identifying the faces of actors and celebrities, almost following Jane's thoughts in the choice and arrangement of the prints.

In this room, where they had spent so many quiet domestic evenings, and had entertained such eminent but respectful guests as Dickens, Tennyson and Browning, Thomas sat alone after Jane's death, night after night, year after year, surrounded by memories of her; and here, in 1881, he died.

The room adjoining was Jane's bedroom. Her 'Red Bed', the four-poster in which she was born, slept for much of her life and was laid after death, shares domination of the room with the portrait of Thomas's mother over the fireplace—a fine Scots face that shows where some of his quality came from. It is not a fussy, feminine room, but, like Jane, orderly and demure. Under glass in this room and its dressing-room are fragile possessions—her belt and lace collar, some of her jewellery, including the ring of linked dolphins she wore on the day she died, scraps of faded writing, locks of hair. The walls are thick with sketches and photographs—one of Nero, the little black and white dog, Jane's 'inseparable companion during eleven years', whose grave is in the pleasant garden one sees from the window. One side of Jane's life in the house is a chronicle of bitter war against the Victorian housewife's enemy, bugs. It is an incredible thought, as one walks through those spotless rooms today, that in Jane's time every wainscot, every bed, might be a lurking-place for them. They are constantly recurring features in the saga of the Carlyles' amazing series of domestics—thirty-four maids in thirty-two years, not counting temporary helps. There was almost no accident or misdemeanour beyond their scope: drunkenness, violence, 'little misfortunes' (one of them born in the back dining-room while Thomas was taking tea with a lady visitor in the front one), lies, thieving, china-smashing and falls. The kitchen, then so cheerless, now a charming living-room, was the home by day and night of these girls. Their wages were pathetically small, but for Jane they nearly all seemed to have a devoted affection that withstood her scoldings.

The top floor of the house is all Thomas, for this is the attic study he designed as a sound-proof room where he could write in peace, free from the acoustic agonies inflicted on him by neighbours and their fowls. It was a complete failure. Through its skylight came all sorts of other distracting sounds he had never noticed before. 'The noisiest room in the house,' Jane pronounced it. But Thomas used it as a study for twelve years, and wrote *Frederick the Great* in it. Its cases, walls and bookshelves hold countless reflections of the man, his mind and his works—books, autograph letters, portraits, busts, prints, manuscripts. There is a unique scrap of manuscript, salvaged after the first volume of *The French Revolution* had been burnt to ashes by a too diligent housemaid and heroically rewritten, in a new form. '*That* first volume could not be written again, for the spirit that animated it is past; but another first volume I will try.'

Yet, although Thomas Carlyle, the man, is clearly present in the room, the author is elusive, for we are conscious that the works that flowed from the great and serious mind are now gathering dust on library bookshelves. He was revered in his lifetime: 'I would go at all times farther to see Carlyle than any man alive,' said Dickens. He was an inspiration to Ruskin, Keir Hardie and the early Socialists. Then he became a memory of an arresting figure seen about Chelsea in the wide-brimmed hat that still hangs in his hall; then a statue on the Embankment. Now he lives on largely through his house, and his wife.

In the many portraits and photographs of Thomas and Jane there is all their married life, with its underlying melancholy. In her pocket-book, Jane had written prophetically:

In Friendship's arms each heart reposes;
There soul to soul pours out its woe;
My lips an oath forever closes,
My sorrows God alone can know.

And there is a line inscribed on a decorated box in the drawing-room: 'Lennoxlove, 1825. All was rapture then, which is but missing now.'

There had been an earlier sweetheart than Thomas, a broken engagement. But that she loved Thomas greatly there is no doubt. Her mysterious illnesses, which change her in her portraits from a smiling young beauty into a grey-haired woman with the shadow of death and fear of madness in her face, owed much to deep, if subconscious, frustration. Thomas often briskly told her that the cure for her troubles was work. In the first half of the nineteenth century there was no work she could do, other than household management, except for the work she might have done, and did not. Thomas's letters are good, but hers are superb. She was in fact a born author. At her last meeting with Dickens she had given him the first part of a plot for a novel, which deeply impressed him. After her sudden death he reflected: 'No one now to finish it. None of the writing women come near her. . . .'

Thomas himself had unknowingly summed up his wife when he said of Coleridge that the poet was 'a melancholy instance of a genius running to waste'.

But her immense humour, as well as her sadness, is in the house. She who loved cleanliness and order would rejoice to see it now, shining as home-made beeswax polish could never make it; would revel in the garden where she planted so much that was to live on after her, and in the transformed old kitchens. And she would cherish the small dog who follows Nero's old walks, and sleeps in Nero's places, and is called Thomas.

DICKENS HOUSE

Doughty Street, Bloomsbury, London

CHARLES DICKENS 1837–1840

DOUGHTY STREET was a splendidly exclusive place to live in 1837. The wide street of tall Georgian houses was shut off at each end by gates and the forbidding presence of a watchman. Gray's Inn lay to the south of it, the Foundling Hospital to the north. It was with pride and pleasure that young Mr and Mrs Charles Dickens, baby Charley and Mrs Dickens's sister Mary moved into the twelve-roomed house, No. 48, during the last weekend of March. Dickens referred in a letter to 'the worry and turmoil of moving', but his orderly nature and delight in new places must have made the settling-in period a happy time for his family.

Doughty Street is still a quiet, dignified thoroughfare, though the gates have gone and the watchman has long since been promoted. The Foundling Hospital has disappeared, with its clock 'lower than most of the rest, and nearer to the ear', that was usually slow, lagging behind the other London chimes 'to strike into the vibration alone'. Gray's Inn, with its memories of Mr Perker, Mr Phunky and the youthful clerk Dickens, has lost its ancient peace, shaken by the roar of Holborn and the ring of the demolisher's hammer. But 48 Doughty Street remains, and is known as the Dickens House.

The hammers were hovering over it in 1922, when some members of the Council of the Dickens Fellowship stepped in and averted its destruction. They bought it, opened it to the public in 1925, and elected a permanent body of trustees to look after it and retain it in perpetuity as a memorial to Dickens, a library and museum for all Dickensians. And so, of all the houses in which Dickens lived in London, only 48 Doughty Street remains structurally unaltered, and so furnished and arranged that we can reconstruct the life of the young Dickenses in their tenancy of it.

The sturdy door opens, and the visitor stands in the hall; cheerful Pickwickian scenes look down from the walls. The dining-room, with curved doors and wall, is immediately to the left. Its candles were lit and tables spread on the evening of 2nd April 1837, a day or two after they had moved in, for the first anniversary of the marriage of Charles and Kate. They spent a happy evening: Charles sparkling with wit, affection and family pride in his wife and bouncing son; Kate beautiful, languid, already a little slow-going for her dynamic husband; and Mary, seventeen years old, 'young, beautiful and good', 'the grace and life of our home', her brother-in-law called her. Charles's sixteen-year-old brother Fred was there, too, enjoying the general grown-upness of the occasion, and the port.

Now the room is full of relics of this time, and later, dominated by a bust of Dickens in his prime and a grandfather clock with a curious history. It once stood in a coach office at Bath, the property of Moses Pickwick, whose name Dickens borrowed for his immortal character. In the little parlour behind the dining-room Dickens's early love affair with Maria Beadnell is reflected. Maria, disguised as a milkmaid, simpers and languishes at the artist as no doubt she did at the young man who wrote ardent dreadful verse to her:

Life has no charms, no happiness, no pleasures, now for me
Like those I feel when 'tis my lot, Maria, to gaze on thee.

She treated him badly, and he never quite recovered from it. Perhaps it was on the rebound that he married the very different Kate Hogarth. Their marriage licence is here, and the record of their children's births, inscribed by Dickens in the family Bible. There are relics of less fortunate children: the wretched little boys at Greta Hall school in Yorkshire, the original of Dotheboys Hall, and a blacking-pot that recalls Dickens's own youthful slavery at the blacking factory.

A familiar figure is waiting on the first landing. It is the Little Midshipman himself —the very one described in *Dombey and Son* as standing outside Sol Gills's shop to advertise his nautical instruments—which, says Dickens, 'thrust itself out above the pavement, right leg foremost, with a suavity the least endurable, and had the shoe buckles and flapped waistcoat the least reconcileable to human reason, and bore at its right eye the most offensively disproportionate piece of machinery'.

Dickens had no eye for antiques. The Midshipman is in fact a perfectly charming little figure of about 1750, elegant, smart as paint, perhaps the most beautiful object in the Dickens House. He looks towards the door of the drawing-room, which holds a vast Dickens Reference Library, and the desk at which he gave his readings. Here, in the April of 1837, the first visitors to the new house assembled. Richard Bentley, the publisher, left his impression of the evening:

'Dinner in Doughty Street. I the only stranger. Mr Dickens sen., Miss Hogarth, Miss Dickens, the Misses Hogarth. It was a right merry entertainment; Dickens was in force, and on joining the ladies in the drawing-room, Dickens sang two or three songs, one the patter song, "The Dog's Meat Man",

In less than three years' residence here in Doughty Street Charles Dickens wrote his first, freshest novels and came to fame; but he also suffered the traumatic experience that would shadow his life.

and gave several successful imitations of the most distinguished actors of the day. Towards midnight (it was Saturday) I rose to leave, but D. stopped me and pressed me to take another glass of Brandy and water. This I wd. gladly have avoided, but he begged Miss Hogarth to give it me. At the hand of the fair Hebe I did not decline it.'

There were to be parties in plenty, but never again quite such a merry evening. Just a week later 'the fair Hebe' was dead.

From the drawing-room a flight of stairs leads up to the bedroom floor. In the front bedroom slept Charles and Kate, in the smaller back one, Mary. On Saturday, 6th May, they had all come in from the theatre, high-spirited and chattering. Mary seemed perfectly well. There was nothing to prepare Kate and Charles for the violent illness which struck her during the night. In the early afternoon of Sunday she died in Dickens's arms. What caused the tragedy will never be known, for the Births and Deaths Registration Act was not to come into force for a few weeks yet.

Dickens never, in a sense, recovered from this blow. Like Maria Beadnell's rejection, it had a permanent traumatic effect on his sensitive nature. Subconsciously dissatisfied with life by the side of the earthy, too fertile Kate (she was already pregnant again, and miscarried with the shock of Mary's death), he had idealized his young sister-in-law as perfect femininity. Death enshrined her for ever, made her the unreal smiling wax doll without human faults who appears over and over in his novels— Rose Maylie, Little Nell, Agnes. Her portrait is in the bedroom she occupied; she looks plain, long-nosed, slightly rabbit-mouthed, not to be compared with her sister Kate. But the artist (Phiz) may well have maligned her. It was this face that Dickens saw before him all his life, in dream and vision, always beckoning. The only known letter in her handwriting is in this room.

A beautiful Cattermole drawing of Little Nell in the setting of her grandfather's shop hangs above the desk used by Dickens as a lawyer's clerk in Gray's Inn. Perhaps the desk was in his mind when he visualized Bob Cratchit in that tank-like little office, perched on his stool and 'driving away with his pen, as if he were trying to overtake nine o'clock'. We are not told the amount of Bob's weekly wage, but it appears from a page of a petty cash book here that Dickens earned thirteen shillings and sixpence.

The opposite wall is covered with a vast canvas. A lighthouse dominates a seascape of swirling waves, tempestuous sky and storm-wrecked ships. It is in fact a piece of scenery, the act-drop for Wilkie Collins's drama *The Lighthouse*, performed by Dickens's talented amateur theatrical company in 1855. Huge as it is, it took the artist, Clarkson Stanfield, only a couple of mornings to paint. He had been ill, and felt himself past painting large canvases. But Dickens argued with him. 'I would not have this—I declared he must paint bigger ones than ever, and what would he think of beginning upon an act-drop for the proposed vast theatre at Tavistock House?

14

He laughed and caught at this, we cheered him up very much, and he said he was quite a man again.' All his life Dickens could charm almost anyone into almost anything.

In the front bedroom is a painting to which one returns again and again. 'Dickens's Dream', by R. W. Buss, one of the original illustrators of *Pickwick*, shows a contemplative Dickens, his chair drawn back from his desk, the air around him filled with the fairy shapes of his characters, some coloured, some only sketches, for the painting is unfinished. One tiny creature perches on his knee. The picture is a perfect expression in paint of Dickens's almost trance-like state when writing: 'The tale . . . has great possession of me every moment in the day, and drags me where it will.'

His study is on the first floor. In this small room, looking out over a struggling Bloomsbury garden, he wrote his earliest, freshest novels: the end of *Pickwick*, the whole of *Oliver Twist, Nicholas Nickleby*, part of *Barnaby Rudge*. His mind then, and later, can be seen at work in his manuscripts, some of which are here, together with a fine collection of his works as they appeared in monthly parts, and a full set of his first editions. Over the room presides a copy of Maclise's famous portrait of him at twenty-seven, the vivid face—'what a face to meet in a drawing-room!'—turned towards the light, almost feminine in its delicacy yet wholly masculine in the fire and intensity of the expression. The luxuriant brown hair falls to the shining collar of the dandified coat, a strong, slender hand rests on the manuscript as if drawing inspiration from the touch of the paper. 'Here we have the real identical man Dickens,' said Thackeray of this painting; and here we have the young man who lived at 48 Doughty Street at the time of the upspringing of his genius, knowing some poverty, some disappointment, some grief, but nothing of the 'old unhappy loss or want of something' which haunts the bearded, lined face of the later portraits.

During the two years and nine months that the Dickens family lived in this house, Dickens's fame as an author became established. It saw parties, conferences with publishers and illustrators, Dickens and Hogarth family gatherings. Two children were born here, Mamey and Katey, and the house began to shrink. Returning after a summer spent at Petersham and Broadstairs, they found it seemed smaller than before. Kate, never very slender, was putting on weight; perhaps she found the stairs too much for her. House-hunting began again.

Many houses associated with Dickens are still to be seen in various parts of the country. Of them all, the one in Doughty Street is the most extensively preserved as he knew it.

DOCTOR JOHNSON'S HOUSE

City of London

SAMUEL JOHNSON 1749–1759

THOMAS CARLYLE was seeing London, and its literary shrines. Of one he wrote, disgusted at its descent in the world:

'We . . . lately discovered Gough Square, and . . . the very House there, wherein the *English Dictionary* was composed. It is . . . a stout old-fashioned, oak-balustraded house: "I have spent many a pound and penny on it since then," said the worthy landlord: "Here, you see, this Bedroom was the Doctor's study; that was the garden" (a plot of delved ground somewhat larger than a bed-quilt) "here he walked for exercise; these three garret Bedrooms" (where his three Copyists sat and wrote) "were the place he kept his—Pupils in". *Tempus edax rerum!* Yet *ferax* also: for our friend now added, with a wistful look, which strove to seem merely historical: "I let it all in Lodgings to respectable gentlemen; by the quarter or the month; it's all one to me."'

Time, the Eater of Things, has been persuaded to disgorge 17 Gough Square. A succession of less respectable gentlemen brought it down in the world until 1911, when it was rescued and restored to its original state as nearly as possible. In the last war enemy action seriously damaged the garret of *Dictionary* fame. Now the house is whole again. Once a lighthouse of benevolence and high thought, it is now a calm island away from the seething tides of Fleet Street, ignoring alike the distant shrieks of traffic and the rattle of printing-presses.

Here Doctor Johnson came in 1749, after a series of unsatisfactory lodgings. Perhaps Tetty, his beloved wife, temporarily betook herself to the pleasant heights of Hampstead, leaving her husband to deal with the removal, and particularly the setting-up of the Garret for the preparation of his greatest work. He had announced its appearance two years earlier, and had been contracted by five booksellers. Before this date there had been a mysterious gap in the Doctor's life; his career is

Doctor Samuel Johnson spent ten years in this house in Gough Square, off Fleet Street, and reached the zenith of his fame with the publication of his Dictionary.

scantily documented during 1745 and 1746. These are significant years, for they were those of the Jacobite Rebellion led by Prince Charles Edward, and its tragic sequel. Boswell cautiously remarked 'that he had a tenderness for that unfortunate House (of Stuart) is well known; and some may fancifully imagine that a sympathetic anxiety impeded the exertion of his intellectual powers'. Some have fancifully imagined even more, that he was an active Jacobite. It is a romantic but unlikely guess, and Boswell himself concludes that Johnson's zeal had cooled as his reason had strengthened.

No. 17 Gough Square must have pleased the Doctor, though his poor eyesight would prevent him from fully appreciating the beauties that strike us today. It is a graceful, plain, four-square house, built about 1700, its panelling American white and yellow pine. Johnson must have loomed large in it. He was a huge man for his times, five feet eleven in his stockings, according to Mrs Thrale. Fanny Burney considered that 'he has naturally a noble figure; tall, stout, grand and authoritative; but he stoops horribly; his back is quite round . . . his vast body is in constant agitation'. His nervous mannerisms, the *folies de touche* that beset him, his badly fitting, dirty clothes, unhygienic habits (he admitted to Burney that he had 'no passion for clean linen') made him socially difficult. Not, however, socially un-acceptable, for his mighty mind, his amazing wit, his rolling Augustan prose and pontifical pronouncements, had made a strong impact on the literary world of London even by the time he was forty and living at Gough Square. These, and an indefinable quality of likeability which comes to us only in hints; for the eighteenth century was not wont to analyse charm, other than that of a sexual nature. He had a giant's humour, was 'incomparable at buffoonery', was basically kind. 'He was always indulgent to the young, he never attacked the unassuming, nor meant to terrify the diffident,' said his defender Miss Burney.

In January 1749 he had published *The Vanity of Human Wishes* and had seen (imperfectly, so bad were his eyes) his tragedy *Irene* put on at Drury Lane by his ex-pupil David Garrick, whose showy villa he rather envied. Perhaps the comeliness of Gough Square consoled him a little. He settled down there to produce his periodical *The Rambler*, which was written in *Tatler* form and became highly popular. Un-doubtedly much of his time was spent in the Garret, a long, airy room stretching the full length of the house. This, said Boswell from hearsay (they did not meet until 1765), 'he had fitted up like a counting-house . . . in which he gave to the copyists their several tasks'. Five of the copyists were Scotsmen: a tartan thread is conspicuous in the tapestry of Johnson's life.

By 1752 he was fully occupied with the *Dictionary*, fighting down his native, often-deplored 'idleness' to heave his bulk up the slender garret stairs and return once more to the task. The day's labours completed, he would lumber downstairs to the elegant withdrawing-room, where Tetty and tea were awaiting him, the table set with delicate china such as that still kept in the room (though these particular

This long garret was fitted up by Johnson like a 'counting house' for his team of assistants to work on the Dictionary. *The room was restored after Second World War air-raid damage.*

Dresden cups belonged to Mrs Thrale and a later time in Johnson's life). He was 'a lover of tea to an excess hardly credible,' said his biographer Hawkins. 'Whenever it appeared, he was almost raving.' One imagines him beating on frail porcelain with one of the silver teaspoons preserved here, seizing the iron sugar-tongs and throwing in lump after lump.

In March 1752 tragedy struck at 17 Gough Square, for Tetty died. The Widow Porter had been fifty-six at the time of their marriage—twenty-one years older than her bridegroom. His friends could not understand his devotion to her. They called her a nagger—'A clean floor is *so* comfortable,' she would point out to the untidy Samuel—and described her as fat, painted, fond of the bottle to the extent of being 'always drunk', and of doubtful reputation. Against this we know that Johnson adored her with a romantic, almost mystic love, and that his grief at her death was terrible. He prayed, pathetically, 'if Thou hast ordained the Souls of the Dead to Minister to the Living, and appointed my departed Wife to have care of me, grant that I may enjoy the good effects of her attention and ministration whether exercised by appearance, impulses, dreams or in any other manner . . .' And he put her wedding-ring in a little round wooden box, inscribing in it: 'Eheu! Eliz. Johnson, Nupta Jul. 9, 1736, Mortua, eheu! Mart. 17, 1752.'

It was a giant's sigh of grief. Speaking of her in later years, he would add fondly: 'Pretty creature!' Her portrait in the withdrawing-room shows her fair and good-humoured, distinctly handsome, a Restoration lady rather than a Georgian.

Though he had lost Tetty, he now acquired a new companion: Francis Barber, the young Negro servant from Jamaica, recently freed. 'He was in great affliction,' recorded Francis of his master, speaking of this time. Johnson had him well educated and treated him generously and kindly, even after Francis had deserted him; and when the young man rebelled against service in the Navy in 1759 got Tobias Smollett to write to John Wilkes pleading for his release, for 'no man will be a sailor who has connivance enough to get himself into a jail'. 'The Grand Cham of Literature' won his case, and Francis returned to his service.

Another companion, from this time onwards, was Miss Williams, a blind Welsh-woman who had been a friend of Tetty and had attended her deathbed. Again, the Doctor's friends (who seem to have been notable for jealousy) were catty about Miss Williams, calling her peevish, and dirty in her habits. But Boswell thought of her as 'of more than ordinary talents', and her presence must have been a comfort to the widower, now more than ever bedevilled by the black dog of melancholy. The room that was hers faces the withdrawing-room, of which the landing panels are hinged so that one spacious apartment could be made for festive purposes. Alas, there were no such gaieties at Gough Square, nor such an air of quiet elegance as prevails today, disseminated by fine furniture of the period. 'Good books . . . very dusty and in great confusion' lay about; the floor was 'strewed with manuscript leaves', observed Boswell of a later lodging, and so it must have been at Gough Square, where also he kept his 'apparatus for the chymical experiments' which were his hobby. He would lie abed till noon, probably in the room which is now the library, rising tousled and unbathed ('I hate immersion!' he growled). One of a long line of cats would probably share his breakfast. Friends would call, and book-sellers interested in the progress of the *Dictionary*.

At last, in August 1755, it was published in two volumes folio (the first edition can be seen in the dining-room) for the admiration of the world, which, says Bozzy, 'contemplated with wonder so stupendous a work achieved by one man'. Super-seded now by other works, it still makes amazing reading; erudite, exhaustive, startlingly original in the breadth and personal colour of its definitions. 'Excise', for instance, is 'a hateful tax levied upon commodities, and adjudged not by the common judges of property, but wretches hired by those to whom Excise is paid'. Johnson candidly confessed that he was not infallible. Asked why he had wrongly defined the word 'pastern', he replied: 'Ignorance, Madam, pure Ignorance.'

The *Dictionary* brought him fame, but little money at first. He set to work again on a mass of essays and dissertations, thankful that the failing sight of one eye had improved. In 1758 came his new periodical paper *The Idler*. Next year he suffered his second personal loss: his mother died in Lichfield, aged ninety, before her son could visit her. He wrote tenderly to her in her last illness: 'You have been the best mother, and I believe the best woman in the world.' Boswell was told by Strahan the printer that Johnson wrote *Rasselas, Prince of Abyssinia*, to pay for her funeral.

In the spring of 1759 he removed from Gough Square to chambers in Staple Inn, and thence to others until he reached Bolt Court, the house now destroyed by fire, where he reached the zenith of his fame and died in 1784. Of all his residences in the London he loved ('Why, Sir, you find no man at all intellectual who is willing to leave London') only Gough Square remains. Of his possessions few are there, for he neither collected nor left behind him the things of this world. Two—both chairs—bring the man himself before us: one, a fine piece of furniture which the Great Lexicographer begged of his bluestocking friend Elizabeth Carter because he found it so comfortable; the other 'Dr Johnson's dining-chair' from the Old Cock Tavern, grotesquely shaped yet well adapted to hold that vast form.

And so he lumbers down the steps of 17 Gough Square, toward the Thrales, Boswell, Reynolds, and Westminster Abbey....

DOWN HOUSE

Downe, Kent

CHARLES DARWIN 1842–1882

THE *Origin of Species* and *The Descent of Man*, works that revolutionized scientific thinking and rocked the previously firm throne of Victorian piety, were evolved and written in what is still one of the most secluded places in England. The Kentish village of Downe is only a stone's throw from the boundaries of Greater London, but it has changed little in the century and more since Charles Darwin and his family went to live there. The little church they attended stands firmly in its centre; the 'pot-house' where they lodged while house-hunting remains, though dignified to an inn. The winding lane that leads to Down House, the home they took in 1842, is no broader. Pigs root beside it, horses at grass leap and frisk, the fields are wide and fertile.

'The country is extraordinarily rural and quiet with narrow lanes and high hedges . . . it is really surprising to think London is only 16 miles off,' wrote Darwin to his sister. He needed quiet for his scientific studies and for the nervous trouble which beset him all his life. The London house which had been the first home of Charles and his young wife Emma was becoming too small for the growing family. There were two children already and another on the way. Emma perhaps looked back wistfully to the gaieties of London, for she was a gregarious, lively girl, revelling in the parties that made her husband ill and in the theatres he disliked. Determined to make a success of her marriage at all costs, she had turned her back on these pleasures and given up her life to child-bearing and looking after the ailing Charles. He had never been well since the voyage of the *Beagle* brig, from 1831 to 1836, which had been the turning-point of his career; his *Geological Observations* and *Zoology of the Voyage of H.M.S. Beagle* had placed him, at the age of thirty, among the leading scientists of the day.

Emma was disappointed and depressed at the first sight of the house, which Charles had to admit was 'ugly . . . looks neither old nor new', and by its solitary position; nor was her first view of it improved by the fact that she was suffering from severe toothache and headache. Charles liked it, because of its 'capital study', large rooms and quantity of bedrooms available for family, domestics and visitors: Emma was not only wife but cousin, one of the great Wedgwood family of Staffordshire, an

Charles Darwin formulated his evolutionary theories and wrote The Origin of Species *and many other works during forty years spent in his remote Kentish home.*

affectionate and united clan. He liked the cherry and walnut trees, the magnolia and mulberry whose presence might mean that the place was not too cold in winter, but doubted the capabilities of soil full of chalk flints. He paid about two thousand pounds for the house, considering it a bargain, and the family moved in on 14th September. Though its façade is plain enough, time has mellowed it into a kind of grace. The main structure belongs to the late eighteenth century. The Darwins' improvements included a new study and a drawing-room with veranda.

One enters now the original hall, small, hung with decorous religious prints; and there, in bronze effigy, the familiar bearded figure leans back in a chair, as in a throne of knowledge, slumped and sagacious. Behind him, let into a pane of glass, are the scribbled signatures of two eighteenth-century children: his famous grandfather, Erasmus Darwin, and sister Susannah. Erasmus, that powerful personality, is to be met with all over Down House, in portrait, letter rhyme and treatise.

On the left of the inner hall a door leads to the New Study, intended by Charles to be an improvement on his old work-place, but only used for the last two years of his life. Now it is a cheerful room dedicated to a pictorial exposition of 'The Grand Darwinian Theory', of which Victorian students sang:

> *Your attention, ladies—let me win it;*
> *Just think of this theory for a minute,*
> *Is there really not something distressing in it,*
>   *To think you sprang from a monkey?*
> *That delicate hand was a monkey's paw,*
> *Those lovely lips graced a monkey's jaw . . .*
> *Those sparkling eyes a monkey did lend,*
> *From a monkey you borrowed this Grecian bend,*
>   *By this grand Darwinian Theory.*

On the brightly coloured walls charts and illustrations tell the story of Evolution, a dramatic single sentence heading it: 'The earth began as a whirling mass of hot gases . . .' Sounding names follow each other—Cambrian, Silurian, Triassic, Jurassic. Primeval things come up from primeval slime, swimming or crawling; the great lizards browse, fight and die. Ape-man rears unsteadily on hind legs, and begins to co-ordinate hands and brain, to be followed by Man himself. It is a triumphant progress, brilliantly deduced by Charles Darwin from intensive studies which brought him to the conclusion that in all living organisms the characteristics of offspring are determined by the process of natural selection, which eventually produces something quite different from the original ancestors. 'We may safely infer that not one living species will transmit its unaltered likeness to a distant futurity. . . . And as natural selection works solely by and for the good of each being, all corporeal and mental endowments will tend to progress towards perfection.'

He wrote these words and the rest of *The Origin of Species*, published in 1859, in the old study, which lies to the left of the inner hall. In every respect, even to a pervasive smell of chemicals, it appears to be still in use. On a library table is a motley collection of objects that led to the *Origin*. Pill-boxes, labelled in minute writing, contain dried beetles and small insects. Small bottles still hold their chemical contents, with here and there a warning: 'POISON. Potassio-ferrous cyanide'. Fossils, flints and chalk formations (some of them from the kitchen garden he had distrusted), a prism, a flask of oil, were all the humble instruments of his great research. His microscope is on the window-sill, beside it the revolving, wheeled stool he used for propelling himself effortlessly about the room on his weaker days. In a screened-off corner are the bath, wash-stand and chamber-pot he kept here, so that he might waste as little time and energy as possible going up and down the stairs. On the desk where he wrote his works are two of them—a *Memoranda of Vegetation* and a *Monograph on the Fossil Balanidae and Verrucidae*. For nearly forty years he worked

The old study at Down House and its contents are still as they were when Darwin thought, experimented and wrote here. Few rooms in the world have seen more profoundly influential work achieved in them.

here, dissecting, analysing, thinking and writing: it is perhaps one of the most important rooms in the world.

The old dining-room, next to the study, has become the Erasmus Darwin Room, set out with signs and tokens of the famous naturalist and philosopher, whose genes had obeyed his grandson's theory by descending in an altered and improved form. His portrait by Joseph Wright of Derby, one of his patients, shows a large, genial man, capable of such frivolities as the 'Letter to Miss Seward's Cat' which one can read in a show-case. The owner of Dear Miss Pussy, something of a beauty, had hoped to marry Dr Erasmus, but he had chosen elsewhere; so Anna Seward, the Swan of Lichfield, bluestocking and poetess, narrowly escaped being Charles Darwin's grandmother. One wonders what the genetic result might have been.

A gentle piece of irony shares the showcase with Miss Seward and Pussy. It is a set of verses by Dr Darwin, an 'Ode on the Folly of Atheism'. 'Dull Atheist!' sharply observes the Doctor,

> Could a giddy dance
> Of atoms lawless hurl'd,
> Construct so wonderful, so wise,
> So harmoniz'd a world?

Well, perhaps not quite lawless, his grandson may have reflected.

The new dining-room, at the back of the house, is full of Darwin treasures and relics. Besides a model of the *Beagle*, there are its log and Darwin's notebooks of the voyage (the foundations of his later studies), an excited young man's record of a strange, unparalleled trip.

Another case contains feminine, charming things: two botanical fans, a lock of Emma's golden-brown hair, a fairer lock, set in a brooch, from the head of her daughter Anne Elizabeth, who died, aged nine, in 1851. Of ten children, they were to lose three, ironic demonstration of Darwin's theory that over-population, by the law of Nature, is virtually impossible. The children who survived seem to have had a remarkably happy and free life, and to have been very close to their parents. No stern patriarch ruled at Down; Charles was as instinctive a father as Emma was a mother, and their offspring fully repaid their un-Victorian tolerance. Their portraits, painted soon after their marriage, show countenances equally blended of good nature and good sense, and there is a distinct family likeness between them. Charles had thought his own face far too 'ugly' to win such a girl as Emma Wedgwood. His daughter Henrietta wrote; 'He had the strange idea that his delightful face, so full of power and sweetness, was repellently plain.' But he need not have worried. Emma was in love with him, and seems to have remained so all her life.

His older image, in flowing beard, cloak and wideawake, looks down on cases that hold such intimate and sad relics as his daily health notes, and recipes for a healthy life: 'Breakfast, 1 cup of cocoatina, slowly sipped'. It is not very surprising that his diet benefited him little.

The most curious item here is an immensely detailed Darwin pedigree. The names it includes are fantastically famed, nearly every noble family in England contributing —Beauchamp, Ferrars, de Stafford, Howard, Knollys, Paget—while farther back are Frankish and Scots kings, even Alfred the Great. As an exercise in heredity it is almost unmatched.

The leisure hours of the family were passed in the new drawing-room at the back of the house, one of those added by the Darwins. It is a fine, light, spacious room, looking out on to the pleasant gardens. Emma would rest on her sofa, which is still in the room: in courtship days Charles had dreamed of 'a nice soft wife on a sofa, with good fire and books and music perhaps'. Reading to him was a particular accomplishment of hers; and when she played for him on her Broadwood piano, which still stands by the window, her music-canterbury beside it, his dream was amply fulfilled.

Charles Darwin died at Down House on 19th April, 1882, aged seventy-four. After long years of semi-neurotic and undiagnosed ailments, angina had caught up with him. He wrote letters and made experiments to the last, his last work being a note to the periodical *Nature* on 'The Dispersal of Bivalves'. The odium attached to his demolition of the Old Testament view of Creation had largely disappeared, and they buried him, not in Downe churchyard where he had hoped to lie beside his brother, but in Westminster Abbey. Emma followed him in 1896, but was buried in the little churchyard of Downe. She had spent her last summer as she would have wished, cheerful, active, surrounded by grandchildren, and still reading Charles's *Journal*. 'It gives me a sort of companionship with him which makes me feel happy,' she told Henrietta.

After they were gone, Down House became a school, fell empty again and began to decay. It was preserved by the efforts of the British Association for the Advancement of Science, and by funds provided by the London surgeon Sir George Buckstone Browne. Back to the house, from the generous hands of descendants and friends, came Darwin possessions, manuscripts, pictures and relics. Administered today by the Royal College of Surgeons, it remains as he knew it, the place that gave him forty years of seclusion for his studies, land for his experiments and very great domestic happiness.

A diorama of Mulberry Harbour at Port Arromanches on D-Day plus 109—23rd September 1944—dominates one wall of Sir Winston Churchill's library at Chartwell.

CHARTWELL MANOR

Westerham, Kent

WINSTON SPENCER CHURCHILL 1922–1965

ONE DAY in 1922 a family party drove into Kent in an old Wolseley car. They passed through the village of Westerham, birthplace of the hero of Quebec, and ascended the long, twisting hill overlooking the Weald, the heart of the 'Garden of England'. After a few more minutes' drive between massed ancient trees and great rhododendrons, the car pulled up sharply, to turn into the sudden entrance of a small, red-brick manor house.

For the next few hours the visitors roamed everywhere about the deserted, neglected house and explored the vast estate. As they progressed, enthusiasm waxed: until, when it came to the moment to leave, the leader of the expedition had become too excited to remember to switch on the car's ignition and release the handbrake, omissions which were not discovered until a band of willing helpers had pushed the vehicle several hundred yards without avail.

In this way Winston Churchill and his family found and bought Chartwell, their home of homes for the rest of his life: the haven of which he would say, 'Every day away from Chartwell is a day wasted.'

He had needed none of his family's urging to buy it. Whether consciously or not, he had recognized at once in the modest manor which had stood unoccupied for more than a decade a place where he would find relaxation from the pressures of public life, necessary peace for literary composition and occupational therapy in the form of practical work. A smaller man with smaller ideas might have been daunted. Parts of the house dated back to Edward III: it is said that Henry VIII stayed in it on his way to visit Anne Boleyn at Hever. It was not in perfect condition, within or without. Unkempt trees overshadowed windows, creepers threatened walls: there were 82 acres of undeveloped grassland, trees and a small lake.

According to his daughter Sarah, the new owner would at first have been happy to have left the place much as it was. It was his devoted, perceptive wife who lit the fuse which, after a slow-burning start, fired the explosion of practical handymanship which was to bring him so much creative satisfaction, while relaxing him mentally and refreshing his ever-active mind. Soon he was building walls, then cottages, doing much of the work with his own hands with the assistance of a professional mate;

making a swimming pool, complete with a powerful heating installation concealed in a tree trunk; excavating a dam, landscaping an island; not to mention rearing Golden Orfe carp in a shaded pond, painting landscapes and still-lifes out of doors and in the studio he had created, and working on monumental literary projects.

In time the house would grow to contain nineteen bedrooms, eight bathrooms and many other apartments: yet, passing through its front door today, over flagstones which extend on into the entrance hall itself, one finds it surprisingly compact and not at all a reflection of one of the largest of larger than life men. There is drama, but in undertone. The dominant theme is homeliness and warmth, a legacy from Lady Churchill's influence which was such upon both the house and its master that many who came there have testified that Churchill at Chartwell was quite a different being from the belligerent, stubborn warrior of Whitehall.

Perhaps the feature for which the visitor is least prepared is the abundance of colour. Instead of the expected dignity of sombre shades and imposing furniture, there is the harmonic grace of pastel-coloured shades, with a predominance of blue, and a great deal of light, air and modernity. The windows frame living landscapes, and the walls bear Sir Winston's own landscapes and still-lifes, vivid and extrovert, as well as other contemporary artists' works: there is nothing in the way of stern ancestors or dark Old Masters. The long, airy drawing-room, which has heard decades of talk by countless fascinating people, is a symphony in sunshine yellow, taking its colour-note from Lady Churchill's dress in her portrait by Douglas Chandor. The light sparkles in the Lalique cockerel, given to her by General de Gaulle. Beyond its perch, the card table is set ready for the game of bezique, which Sir Winston so much enjoyed.

A cigar box rests beside his place. More ornate cigar boxes appear to have been to Sir Winston what toast racks are to young marrieds: everybody gave him one, from Haile Selassie to the City of Westminster. With the cups won by his racehorses, the crystal bowls shaped like ancient galleys manned by bears and dragons and given to him by Stalin, and countless other gifts, trophies, decorations and awards, they are on show either *in situ* or in the well-designed museum rooms which have had to be created to contain the memorabilia of this man who received so many tokens of the gratitude and esteem of the world. The variety of uniforms to which he was entitled recall his many-sided service, while a wittily arranged selection of his favourite hats for various pursuits remind us, if it were necessary to do so, of the range of facets his character displayed.

The round table of the long, light dining-room is set for tea. Chartwell stands on a slope, so that one descends to this room by a number of stairs, at the foot of which stands a long, low dresser. It was on this that Churchill the artist arranged the bottles depicted in one of his best paintings, 'Bottlescape'. It hangs over the dresser now. This big room, able to hold several score people, judiciously distributed, was where he indulged one of his favourite pastimes, going to the cinema. Staff and all were

Winston Churchill and his family considered this home for over forty years. He declared: 'Every day away from Chartwell is a day wasted.'

invited, if not commanded, to the weekend film show, perhaps of a film provided by its distributors in advance of its general release. He would return to certain favourites again and again: *Lady Hamilton* with Vivien Leigh and Laurence Olivier was one of the chief among them.

Emma's Nelson is permanently present in the form of a small bust on the desk in the study upstairs. A little replica of Napoleon stands a few inches away, amongst the family photographs, the signed picture of Jan Smuts and an effigy of Winston Churchill's favourite kind of dog, a poodle. It is a telltale collection on a surprisingly small desk. There is nothing modest about the room itself, one of the only remaining features of the Edward III structure. Its large floor enabled its owner to pace unconfined under the high roof timbers from which a replica of his Garter Banner hangs. As he paced he dictated, while secretaries, working in half-hour stints, took down his words in shorthand, then hurriedly typed them, barely keeping up with the flow of thought and utterance. He was happiest in this room, working in this way. Generally late at night and in the small hours of morning, he would walk this floor, the unforgettable voice rumbling steadily away as he composed majestic sentences for his books or went over a new speech again and again, listening to his cadences, matching expression and pitch to meaning, until perfection was achieved. This oral method of 'writing' accounts for the matchless quality his prose possesses of making the reader hear the author's voice declaiming to him, insisting on his unflagging attention and participation in the great events and decisions it describes, and recalling its author vividly in every rolling phrase.

It was here, while he inhabited the political wilderness in the 1930's, that he wrote his great ancestral biography, *Marlborough: His Life and Times*, while simultaneously throwing off articles for newspapers and such popular journals as the *Strand Magazine* in order to make money. Much of all his subsequent writings, including those colossal undertakings *The World Crisis*, *The Second World War* and *A History of the English-Speaking Peoples*, were done at Chartwell, so that this study has perhaps seen the composition of more enduring works of history and literature than any other room in the world.

Teams of assistants often helped him, and of course there were, and are, countless books of reference about the place. Yet there are fewer than one might expect, no doubt because their owner's head was a crammed reference library, and what it could not wholly provide an assistant could check and complete. The actual library, on the floor below the study, is quite small, dominated on one side by Frank O. Salisbury's familiar portrait of the war-time Prime Minister, its eyes for ever fixed on the other side of the room, where a large diorama shows Mulberry Harbour at Port Arromanches on D-Day plus 109—23rd September 1944.

Literary genius was only one of Winston Churchill's attributes. Of the authors whose homes have been included in this volume, only he and Philip Sidney are comparable as the possessors of so many qualities of such high order. There is a blood relationship between them: and, more coincidentally, their houses lie not many miles apart. Sidney's time was short, and his memory lives largely in the words of those who felt privileged to know him. Churchill, as brilliant recorder of the world-stirring dramas in which he played a leading role, has set down his own chronicle. One of the most heartfelt passages in it occurs in *The Gathering Storm*, the first volume of his account of the origins and conduct of the Second World War, published in 1948. Describing his decade out of office before that conflict, he relates how he spent the years at Chartwell and pursued practical activities, concluding: 'Thus I never had a dull or idle moment from morning till midnight, and with my happy family around me dwelt at peace within my habitation.'

To visit the house to which he was referring whenever he spoke of 'home' is to come closer to the human soul within the superman.

PENSHURST PLACE

Kent

PHILIP SIDNEY 1554–1586

T HE SIDNEYS are its soul, but it was there long before they came. There was a Manor of Penshurst at the time of the Norman Conquest, when it was granted to the De Pencestres, first of a line of ringing names to be coupled with it. Stephen de Pencestre died and was buried in the chancel of the village church of St John the Baptist. Through his daughter, the manor passed to Sir John De Pulteney, a rich wool merchant who surpassed Whittington by becoming four times Lord Mayor of London. It was he, about 1340, who built the nucleus of the present Penshurst. He intended it to be a fortified manor, but its aspect today is utterly peaceful. The sheep graze languidly; a gardener moves leisurely about the lawns forming a margin between the house and its small, dry moat; cats by the stables wash in the sunshine.

Now the home of Viscount De L'Isle, v.c., Penshurst is open to the public for much of the year, a stately home without gimmicks. Its visitors in the main come to see a beautiful house, interesting contents, a notable garden. Some, however, come because Penshurst was the home of one of the greatest of Englishmen, Sir Philip Sidney.

The house came to the Sidneys in the short reign of Edward VI, who bestowed it on Sir William Sidney, his 'trustye and wellbeloved servant'. He had married Lady Mary Dudley, daughter of the great Northumberland; their 'well-mixed offspring', Philip, was born at Penshurst on 30th November 1554. The Graces smiled on him from the first. His father was handsome and, more rarely in those times, 'of large heart and sweet conversation'. His mother was beautiful until smallpox, caught while nursing Queen Elizabeth, caused her to hide her face beneath a black velvet mask and live in seclusion at Penshurst, where, for this sad reason, there is no portrait of her on the walls. Her son Philip grew, happily enough, along with his brother Robert and sister Frances, learning his lessons from his mother, playing in the great walled garden.

> *Thou hast thy orchard fruit, thy garden flowers,*
> *Fresh as the air, and new as are thy hours . . .*
> *The blushing apricot and woolly peach*
> *Hang on thy walls that every child may reach.*

33

So wrote Ben Jonson while guest at Penshurst of a later Sidney child. Shrewsbury Grammar School took Philip from his home when he was ten, and he met Fulke Greville, his schoolfellow and lifelong friend. Greville, like almost everybody else, was captivated on sight by Philip's peculiar charm: 'Though I lived with him and knew him from a child, yet I never knew him other than a man: with such staidness of mind, lovely and familiar gravity, as carried grace and reverence above greater years. His talk ever of knowledge, and his very play tending to enrich his mind.'

His spell is hard to recapture now, but his pictured face, with its grave, sweet expression, and the quality of his verse, suggest that he was one of those rare souls that come to earth every few centuries or so, of a higher type than the rest of us, with a natural virtue transcending contemporary morals or customs, and with a glowing genius for friendship. Keats, in a later age, is one of those; T. E. Lawrence another; St Francis of Assisi perhaps an earlier one.

This highly civilized character, 'the courtier's, soldier's, scholar's eye, tongue, sword,' at his command, some of the greatest poetry of the Elizabethan age flowing from his pen, only lived to be thirty-two, yet his short life was packed with achievement. Much of it was spent away from Penshurst, travelling abroad with his tutor Languet on the Grand Tour, and as Elizabeth's ambassador, or at the Queen's court of Whitehall, and Wilton, the home of his sister, Lady Pembroke. His *Arcadia* gives a glimpse of Penshurst:

> *. . . built of fair and strong stone, not affecting so much*
> *any extraordinary kind of fineness, as an honourable*
> *representing of a firm stateliness.*

The Kentish landscape seems to be reflected in that of Arcadia.

> *. . . meadows enameled with all sorts of eye-pleasing flowers . . .*
> *the pretty lambs with bleating oratory craved the dams' comfort;*
> *here a shepherd boy piping, as though he should never be old.*

It is impossible to know when and where he wrote the great *Astrophel and Stella* poems, which tell part of the story of his love for Penelope Devereux, to whom he had been betrothed until her sudden marriage with the unpleasant Lord Rich. Why the engagement of Philip and Penelope was broken off will also never be known. Perhaps it was fortunate that they never married and settled down into more prosaic relations, for the lost love became his Stella, unobtainable as Keats's 'Bright Star', for ever celebrated in a series of matchless songs and sonnets.

Her face, one of the loveliest of the sixteenth century, is not at Penshurst; but in the State Dining-Room is a rare portrait of the girl Philip later married, Frances Walsingham, and their daughter. The stiff convention of contemporary portraiture, with its emphasis on clothing and ornament, may not have dealt with Frances very

Penshurst Place—this immaculate example of the less grandiose type of stately home has been the seat of the Sidney family for centuries. The peerless Philip Sidney was born here in 1554.

fairly. Compared with Stella, she is a plain wench, and there is something slightly enigmatic about their marriage.

There are few relics of Philip at Penshurst now, so many possessions and manuscripts having been destroyed in a fire at Wilton. The helmet carried at his funeral, one of the few state funerals in history given to a commoner, is preserved, and a darkened scrap of looking-glass, part of a mirror belonging to him. Everything else has gone as irretrievably as his tomb in Old St Paul's, destroyed in the Great Fire.

Another literary association with Penshurst is recalled by one of the many ancestral portraits on the walls. The most enchanting of all the faces is that of Lady Dorothy Sidney, Philip's niece. She was the 'Sacharissa' of the poet Edmund Waller, who lived not far away and often visited Penshurst as a close family friend. He wrote her verses, good and bad, the best and most famous of them being *Go, Lovely Rose*.

The reluctant lady of those lines was Sacharissa herself. Waller's poetry and passion were not enough for her, and after keeping him in long suspense she became the Countess of Sunderland. Of all Sidney ladies she seems to have been the most gracious, intelligent and (*pace* Waller) sweet-natured. A *Tatler* writer, long after, said of her: 'The fine women they show me nowadays are at best but pretty girls to me, who have seen Sacharissa, when all the world repeated the poems she inspired.'

This book is concerned essentially with the literary features of the houses described, and some of them have indeed little or nothing else to commend them to the visitor. Penshurst is the chief exception. Its history has been so long, and so peopled with high-born folk, that its interest lies on several planes. It has, for instance, the finest remaining baronial hall from the fourteenth century, a vast, towering space where, in the time of Edward III, lord and lady, knight and seneschal, steward, soldier, page, dog-boy and swineherd crowded together in the communal life of a defended manor, while music played in the gallery and smoke swirled from the huge fire in the centre of the floor up to the great chestnut roof, which, its timbers blackened, still remains intact. Edward IV, the White Rose, radiant over the defeat of Lancaster, dined here, and later Henry VIII. Penshurst made an elegant prison for the children of Charles I. There is something of them all to be seen in it, and, even more movingly, the carven figures of ten ordinary men and women of the fourteenth-century household, most of whom would have been wiped out soon afterwards by the Black Death.

Late in the seventeenth century Penshurst fell into danger of decay; but it is to the credit of later owners, not least the present one, that it is to be seen today as an immaculate example of the less grandiose of stately homes. A pleasing thought is that the man who first came to its rescue was Percy Bysshe Shelley's uncle John. Poetry and Penshurst have never been far apart.

SISSINGHURST CASTLE

Kent

VICTORIA SACKVILLE-WEST and HAROLD NICOLSON 1930–

I N 1930 Harold Nicolson and his wife, Victoria Sackville-West, decided that after fifteen years in their small but comfortable fifteenth-century home, Long Barn, near Sevenoaks, Kent, the time had come to look for another country house. Their reason sounds chords familiar today: the farm land next door was going to be 'developed'.

Instead of finding one of those elegant, modernized period houses in a rural setting with which Kent abounds, they bought an uninhabitable ruin, with the prospect of having to spend more than as much again to put it into any semblance of comfortable order.

Nicolson had recently returned from his last diplomatic post, in Germany, and was embarking, with many misgivings, on journalism. His wife had just finished writing what would become her most successful novel, *The Edwardians*, reflecting her girlhood at Knole. Freed from concentration, she was able to search for the new home; and within a few days she had found what she conceived to be ideal. With their schoolboy sons, Ben and Nigel, a secretary and all the family dogs, they inspected the place formally the next day. 'We go round carefully in the mud,' Nicolson recorded in his diary. 'I am cold and calm but I like it.' She had already written in hers: 'Fell flat in love with it.'

They had found (an enterprising estate agent had suggested it, with more hope, one imagines, than optimism) Sissinghurst Castle, two miles from Cranbrook in the Weald of Kent. It was not a castle; and those parts of it that had not been demolished for their materials were in ruins. As long before as 1752, Horace Walpole had visited it, and found 'a park in ruins and a house in ten times greater ruins'.

There had been a house at Saxingherste as early as the twelfth century. New owners had pulled the place down at the beginning of the sixteenth, leaving only the moat of the original ground scheme. They built a large new house, in the Elizabethan three-sided fashion, which began to share the family's decline in the mid seventeenth century. No longer wanted as a family home, it was leased to the government. Doors and windows were sealed, and several hundred French seamen, captured during the Seven Years War, were marched in. In due course there were some three thousand prisoners at Sissinghurst, and the place had acquired the reputation of a hell-hole. Edward Gibbon, the future historian, then doing service with the Hampshire Militia, was one of the guards in 1760. He recorded: 'The duty was hard, the dirt most oppressive . . .' The prisoners, harshly guarded and hungry, in cold, filthy rooms, protested in vain; so they burnt all the woodwork for firewood and smashed everything of no use to them. Besides reducing the house to a shambles they unconsciously dignified it in name: from their habit of referring to it as 'le château' it became, and remains, Sissinghurst Castle. Most of it was pulled down by subsequent private owners, the only inhabitants until 1930 being farm labourers, living poorly in the ruins.

When the Nicolsons found it, it had been used for many years as a rubbish dump. Tin cans, broken bedsteads, rusted farm implements and piles of long-decayed vegetable roots lay everywhere. All that remained of the buildings were a low range of about 1490 which had been converted in Victorian times into the parish workhouse; the Elizabethan brick tower, standing apart; and a cottage, once the end of the long Elizabethan south wing. Vita Sackville-West wrote later: 'Yet the place, when I first saw it on a spring day in 1930, caught instantly at my heart and my imagination. I fell in love; love at first sight. I saw what might be made of it. It was Sleeping Beauty's Castle: but a castle running away into sordidness and squalor; a garden crying out for rescue. It was easy to foresee, even then, what a struggle we should have to redeem it.'

Visitors to Sissinghurst Castle today can only imagine the struggle; for the result is so perfect that the buildings seem to have been in constant occupation, while the vast and varied gardens are amongst the finest in England. Over a period of years the Nicolsons and, during holidays from Eton, their boys paid working visits of a few days' duration, living in gum-boots, sleeping on camp-beds in the one habitable room of the tower and eating cold food. Harold Nicolson revealed an unexpected talent for garden design, complemented perfectly by his wife's practical knowledge. 'Profusion, even extravagance and exuberance, within the confines of the utmost linear severity,' was their guiding principle in reshaping the wilderness into gardens which combine the dignity of formal design with the inspired appeal of informal planting. The former stable changed into a vast library; a granary was made into accommodation for the boys; the cottage became the Nicolsons' living quarters and Harold Nicolson's work-place; and the first-floor room in the tower was annexed by Vita Sackville-West as her sitting-room and study.

Sissinghurst is now the home of the Nicolsons' youngest son, Nigel, and his family. He made it over to the National Trust in 1966, since when it has been attracting even greater numbers of visitors than it did before. The gardens have been open to the public for some years, for, although Vita Sackville-West was anything but a gregarious, out-going person, she was proud of her creation and liked people to come and admire it. She would come out to talk with them sometimes, able to do so

A squalid prison for French seamen in the Seven Years War, the sixteenth-century 'castle of Sissinghurst' was a ruin when Harold Nicolson and Vita Sackville-West bought it in 1930. They transformed it into a much visited showplace.

Flowers always adorn the desk where Vita Sackville-West worked in her sanctum in the Elizabethan tower. The photograph is of one of her few close friends, Virginia Woolf.

because she knew that it was her right to break off the conversation at whatever point she wished and return to her privacy. People about the place did not distract her. She was not a writer of routine habits like her husband. He, with his Foreign Office background, displayed obvious unease if kept from his typewriter during working hours. She, of the poetic temperament, would happily potter in the garden at any hour until, in her own good time, she would drift to her room and begin to work. Equally she would remain there until she had done all she wished: oblivious to time, to hunger, to cold, to discomfort. Often she would work in the unheated room until the small hours of the morning. Domestic affairs meant little or nothing to her. She resented the implication of inferiority in womanhood, and always wished she had been a male. At her death, her son records, she was found to possess one evening dress, which no one could remember having seen her wear. It was thirty-five years old. Her world was the poet's, the novelist's, the gardener's; and she achieved great things in all three spheres.

The room has been preserved as she left it when she died in 1962. It is a work room most writers would envy: isolated in the tower, lit by windows from which, she used to say, she could see without being seen, lined with books of reference, mainly about English literature, history and travel, especially in Italy, and gardening. A photograph of one of her few close friends, Virginia Woolf, is on her desk beside ones of the Brontë sisters and Harold Nicolson. Within arm's reach of her chair are still the books she used in writing her last biographical work, *Daughter of France*.

Although her best works, the novel *The Edwardians* and the long poem *The Land*, were finished before ever she saw Sissinghurst, she composed in this room such fine things as *The Dark Island, Pepita, Saint Joan of Arc, The Garden* and the poem *Sissinghurst*.

Harold Nicolson's own Sissinghurst books include *Diplomacy* and the revised *Peacemaking*, and his notable biographies of George V, Curzon and Dwight Morrow. But a work surpassing any other Sissinghurst writing is the diary which Harold Nicolson kept without a break from 1929 until 1964. Every day after breakfast he recorded, on one of his three typewriters (named Rikki, Tikki and Tavi), the events and thoughts of the previous day. The loose sheets of paper were then consigned to a filing cabinet and almost never looked at again. Ultimately there were some three million words, seen by nobody else, written with no specific intention and certainly not with thought of publication.

Now edited by Nigel Nicolson, himself an author and publisher, Harold Nicolson's diaries and the letters between him and his wife constitute a brilliant reflection of the years they span and what must be a unique record of a marriage. Despite the numerous and considerable differences between the couple in temperament and inclinations, they achieved perfect understanding. Their devotion is mirrored not only in their words but in their restoration of the home they loved. The expression 'Another quiet day at Sissinghurst' was a standing family joke of the Nicolsons: it was also their ideal.

LAMB HOUSE

Rye, Sussex

HENRY JAMES 1897–1916

A. C. and E. F. BENSON 1918–1940

IN 1896 Henry James was in his early fifties, a bachelor, and famous. Such works as *Portrait of a Lady*, *The Europeans*, *Washington Square*, *The Bostonians* and *The Princess Casamassima* had established him in the eyes of readers on both sides of the Atlantic as the 'interpreter of his generation': especially that generation of his fellow Americans who had 'discovered' Europe. Like many of them, he had chosen to make Europe his home; though instead of Florence or Paris, he had opted for England.

He lived in London. In a typically English fashion—although officially still an American citizen—he generally took his summer holidays at some such genteel seaside resort as Bournemouth or Torquay. But this year he went into Sussex, to occupy a friend's cottage overlooking the ancient and picturesque Cinque Port of Rye. He found the town itself attractive, but one feature of it irresistible. This was a red-brick house of Georgian construction but much longer history, occupying a watchful position at the bend of the cobble-stoned West Street, its long, high garden wall broken by an appealing garden room, jutting out into and above the street at right angles to the house itself. It was this unusual feature, seen in a coloured sketch at a friend's house in London, that had prompted James to stroll across and, as he put it, 'to make sheep's eyes at it, the more so that it is called Lamb House'.

He was enchanted and longed to occupy the house. There seemed little hope of that, since it was in family occupation. Still, before leaving Rye the envious author left his name and his hopes with a friendly ironmonger, who, little more than a year later, transmitted the unexpected news that the house was Henry James's for the asking. The owner had died suddenly; his son preferred the golden frenzy of the Yukon to the peace of Rye; James could have Lamb House on a long lease at 'terms quite deliciously moderate'. He accepted at once. After he had been in occupation only two years he was offered the freehold, again at a most reasonable figure, and became the proud owner.

'There are two rooms of complete old oak—one of them a delightful little parlour, opening by one side into the little vista, church-ward, of the small old-world street, where not one of the half-dozen wheeled vehicles of Rye ever passes; and on the

Henry James was enchanted by the house during a chance visit to Rye in 1896. Chance made him its owner soon after, and it was his favourite home for nearly twenty years.

other straight into the garden and the approach, from that quarter to the garden-house aforesaid, which is simply the making of a most commodious and picturesque detached study and workroom,' he wrote to his sister-in-law.

There were other rooms, equally charming when redecorated, and about an acre of lawn and mature garden, bounded by the old wall on which long-established fruits flourished. 'The house is really quite charming enough in its particular character, and as to the stamp of its period, not to do violence to by rash modernities; and I am developing under its inspiration the most avid and gluttonous eye and most

43

infernal watching patience in respect of lurking "occasions" in not-too delusive Chippendale and Sheraton,' he declared in that prolix style which characterized both his writing and his speech.

When, in 1950, twenty-four years after Henry James's death, the house was presented to the National Trust, the contents which his 'infernal watching patience' had enabled him to amass were not given with it, but were sold at public auction. A few years ago Lamb House acquired as tenant a distant kinsman of Henry James, the author H. Montgomery Hyde, who has since managed to retrieve many items. Others have returned through the Trust and from generous donors, so that Lamb House today, if not just as James knew it, has a charm which reflects truly what he termed that 'quiet essential amiability' which made him return there gratefully after every enforced absence.

Only one principal feature is no more: the garden-house which a German bomb destroyed in 1940. In the warmer months he worked in it, dictating steadily to his secretary, wandering to the window to gaze down at some passer-by while grasping for the exact word or seeking the logical ending for one of his meandering sentences. When the weather grew cool he transferred to the cosier Green Room, on the first floor of the house itself, where his ruminative view was of the lawn, an ancient mulberry tree, now no more, and many roses: a vista which delighted him by its very Englishness. In these surroundings he wrote some of his best novels and tales, among them *The Wings of the Dove*, *The Golden Bowl* and *The Ambassadors*. Lamb House served as the model for Mr Longdon's in *The Awkward Age*, and is the setting for the ghost story *The Third Person*.

James was himself the very model of a literary gentleman of high eminence: large, stout, dignified, rather pompous, yet with touchingly absurd little affectations and mannerisms. He was a familiar figure in Rye, out with his little dog for his regular afternoon stroll, his hat, gloves and stick selected precisely from the collection which always lay on the table in the fine entrance hall, according to whether his footsteps were to bend towards the surrounding Romney Marsh, or to the golf club, or on a round of calls about the town. In the evening he would work again, unless there were guests in the house. There were many visitors in the course of a year, including such literary colleagues as Chesterton, Belloc, Conrad, Max Beerbohm, Kipling and Walpole. He took an almost child-like delight in showing off his beloved house and garden to them. So many of us soon take for granted that which we once coveted: not so Henry James with Lamb House. As age and ill health hemmed him in, restricting his movement and making him spend more time in London, farther from the hard winters of the Marsh and closer to his heart specialist, he yearned anew for 'the blessed, the invaluable, little old refuge-quality of dear L.H.'.

He asked to be taken there in his last illness, but it was not feasible. He died, a British citizen at last, in February 1916, having been just sufficiently conscious to recognize that the insignia they brought to his bed was the Order of Merit.

Henry James wrote of the 'quiet essential amiability' of the elegant Lamb House: but it is familiar to readers of a later owner, E. F. Benson, as the home of that most unamiable spinster, 'Miss Mapp'.

Through his nephew, Henry James, jnr., the house soon passed into the joint tenancy of two notable authors who had been frequent visitors, the brothers E. F. and A. C. Benson. A. C., Master of Magdalene College, Cambridge, occupied Lamb House during the university vacations, and in the comparatively short time spent there until his death in 1925 wrote several volumes of fiction and memoirs. E. F. Benson, who had hitherto lived in the house only when his brother was absent, enjoyed full occupation for fifteen more years, dying in 1940. During that time he brought Lamb House a new, though to most people anonymous, celebrity, as 'Mallards', the home of his abominable fictional spinster Elizabeth Mapp, the central figure of a frequently reprinted series of comic novels, including *Miss Mapp, Our Lucia, Trouble for Lucia* and others.

45

Rye, whose river is the Tillingham, is confessedly the 'Tilling' of these delightful books, peopled with characters epitomizing the snobberies, jealousies and petty machinations of an English parochial society. In the Preface to the first of them, Benson wrote: 'I lingered at the window of the garden-room from which Miss Mapp so often and ominously looked forth. To the left was the front of her house, straight ahead the steep cobbled way, with a glimpse of the High Street at the end, to the right the crooked chimney and the church. The street was populous with passengers, but search as I might, I could see none who ever so remotely resembled the objects of her vigilance.'

Although there is today only a commemorative tablet in place of the garden-room where Henry James dictated and Miss Mapp contrived her catty schemes, the picture of Lamb House is at once recognizable. Whether or not the residents of Rye identified themselves (or, more likely, each other) in the townsfolk of 'Tilling', the maliciously observant author continued to enjoy their respect: they elected him their mayor three years running.

BATEMAN'S

Burwash, Sussex

RUDYARD KIPLING 1902–1936

IT IS the house of *They*. In that incomparably haunting story, Rudyard Kipling chose the neighbourhood of Washington, Sussex, for the house which the traveller discovered at the end of a track that appeared to lead to nowhere. There is no such house near Washington; but it is impossible to approach Bateman's, near Burwash, without feeling that here *is* 'Hawkin's Old Farm', where lived the blind woman who had gathered about her the souls of dead children.

Here are the 'carpeted ride', the great still lawn, the yews which, in the traveller's day, were clipped into the shape of horsemen, ten feet tall; and 'the ancient house of lichened and weather-worn stone, with mullioned windows and roofs of rose-red tile'.

The reason for the poignancy of *They* lies at Bateman's. Kipling came here in 1902, three years after the death at six years old of his eldest child, Josephine. In the house of the dream-children the bereaved father in the story found his lost child again; and for Kipling, Josephine, though she died in America, must have been here always, unseen but present and dear.

This is the home that Kipling had sought for years. He was thirty-six when he came here, with the fame of his great Indian stories and his poems around him. He and his American wife, Caroline Starr Balestier, had lived in her native country for some years, but now they wanted to settle permanently in England, in 'a real House for keeps'.

It was in Kipling's alarming Locomobile, known as Jane Cakebread Lanchester—Kipling was one of the earliest motorists—that he and Caroline came to Bateman's, and, seeing the house, cried: 'That's her! The Only She! Make an honest woman of her—quick!'

They had previously suffered from a house with a bad Feng Shui—'Spirit of the House'—which had produced in them 'a gathering blackness of mind'. But at Bateman's the Feng Shui was good, Kipling decided on entering: 'No shadow of ancient regrets, stifled miseries, nor any menace, though the "new" end of her was three hundred years old.'

The house lay in a remote valley, not particularly accessible from the little village of Burwash. It had peace and great beauty and was highly favourable to writing.

'That's her! The Only She!' cried Rudyard Kipling and his wife when their house-hunting ended at Bateman's in 1902. The house has poignant associations with some of his finest stories.

Kipling, no longer preoccupied with the East, became a teller of English tales and a singer of English songs. Bateman's is the house of *Puck of Pook's Hill* and *Rewards and Fairies*, stories of history and legend that grew naturally from the beautiful, mysterious Sussex landscape that surrounded the house: 'the woods that know everything and tell nothing'.

Bateman's stands golden and beautiful in its fine formal gardens, which seem to grow naturally from the countryside, yet make a perfect setting for the house. 'Like a beautiful cup on a saucer to match,' a member of the Kipling family put it. Sussex ironmasters built it and lived there in the early seventeenth century. Kipling mentioned them, the Collins family, in the story *Hal o' the Draft*. Hal tells Dan and Una how, in the days of Elizabeth and the first James, 'the valley was as full o' forges and fineries as a May shaw o' cuckoos'. A handsome fireback in an upper room at Bateman's shows an ironmaster of the period.

From the garden a deep porch, carved with Kipling initials, leads into the large hall where Kipling used to take tea and chat with farm bailiffs, neighbours and distinguished visitors; for, as he said, 'sooner or later all sorts of men cast up at our house'. Fine Jacobean panelling is here, and the first relics of Kipling's India that the visitor will see: mantelpiece brasses and an Indo-Chinese chest said to have belonged to the last King of Oudh.

On the right of the entrance, the small but impressive dining-room is hung with a remarkable wall-covering of Cordova painted leather, once of dazzling silver but now tarnished with age. In the drawing-room, where there hangs a painting of Rudyard Lake, in Staffordshire, the origin of Kipling's Christian name, the furniture waits as if for the family to return. The house's contents have been preserved and arranged so that Kipling would still find everything in its old place.

A noble staircase leads to the upper floor. Half way up it John Collier's portrait of Kipling compels the visitor to halt with its steady gaze. Other portraits and a bronze bust grouped near here make his personality even more dominant than in the downstairs rooms. The spectacled eyes follow one everywhere, humorous, kindly, yet strangely stern: the eyes of 'a master mariner who has kept long night watches upon perilous seas'.

Kipling's study is one that any author could envy: large, light, airy, and with a whole library of reference works lining sagging shelves from floor to ceiling. The enormous table at which he wrote still has his 'writing tools' laid out on it, though, to judge by his own reference to it, rather more tidily than he would have known:

'I always kept certain gadgets on my work-table, which was ten feet long from North to South and badly congested. One was a long, lacquer, canoe-shaped pen-tray full of brushes and dead "fountains"; a wooden box held clips and bands; another, a tin one, pins; yet another, a bottle-slider, kept all manner of unneeded essentials from emery-paper to small screw-drivers; a

Kipling's study at Bateman's is as he left it: his chair raised on blocks, 'writing tools' in readiness, big waste-paper basket awaiting the endless drafts and revisions which littered his way to perfection.

paper-weight, said to have been Warren Hastings'; a tiny, weighted fur-seal and a crocodile sat on some of the papers; an inky foot-rule and a Father of the Penwipers which a much-loved housemaid of ours presented yearly, made up the main-guard of these little fetishes.'

Most of them are there today, even down to the little fur-seal. His blotting-paper bears the shadow of his handwriting, and the pewter inkpot the shadow of his small vanity, in the form of the titles of his works, scratched by him into the metal. Beneath the desk stands a telling reminder of his professionalism, a vast, woven waste-paper basket, large enough to receive the endless drafts and revisions which littered his progress towards perfection. His walnut writing chair stands on blocks, so that he could sit in perfect comfort. It is drawn up ready for work, and pipe and pipe-cleaners lie ready to hand. Above the mantelpiece hangs Sir Philip Burne-Jones's painting of Mrs Kipling. There are photographs of Josephine and of Kipling's father. A showcase contains such treasures as pieces of the *Victory*'s bunting and the iron-work pen-case mentioned in *Kim*. There is room in this study, as there was in its owner's life, for more than the preoccupations of his trade.

Next to the study is a large room now used for exhibitions. It contains the fireback showing the Sussex ironmaster, and eight plaques by Kipling's father, a skilful artist, illustrating stories from his son's books.

Down in the garden the yews have stood sentinel since the year Kipling came to Bateman's. Most of the pleasing garden effects were created by the Kiplings them-selves, making use of flowering shrubs and rare trees, though a white willow, with an enormous circumference, is possibly more than three centuries old. A large inviting lily pond is the same in which their children and their friends used to bathe and row in small boats. Children were always welcomed at Bateman's. They take to it strangely when they visit it today.

Through the garden gate is a wild garden containing the graves of family pets; and at the end of it is the Dudwell trout stream where Kipling used to fish in 'a sort of thick, sleepy stillness smelling of meadow-sweet and dry grass'. It is the Friendly Brook of *A Diversity of Creatures*, and the old mill near by is to be found in *Traffics and Discoveries*.

On a sundial in the garden Kipling engraved the words 'It is later than you think'. Close to it is the original stone which marked his grave in Westminster Abbey. He died at Bateman's, aged seventy, on 18th January 1936.

CLOUDS HILL

Wool, Dorset

T. E. LAWRENCE 1923–1935

IN THIS region of surprises a main road abruptly becomes a topless tunnel of giant rhododendrons: a seemingly aimless track leads to a nuclear power station: a seaward highway skirts unexpectedly the foot of the Iron Age earthwork, Maiden Castle, itself astoundingly huger than anticipated.

Then there is that other road which turns out of lush Dorsetshire greenery into a shadeless desert of raw, yellow and white clay, all ridges and depressions with surfaces trampled hard and scored by what look uncommonly like tank tracks. Yes, we think: not unlike a real desert remembered in the Middle East after tank warfare; and at that moment there is a clattering roar, and the dark green snout of some armoured vehicle of a kind unfamiliar to us rears up monstrously over one of the ridges. It hangs momentarily, then topples, to go jauncing off at high speed in the direction of a distant ugliness which can only be a military establishment.

We are soon told by notices that all this is Bovington Camp, the headquarters of the Royal Tank Regiment, formerly the Tank Corps: and we know that we shall have to turn and drive back one mile northward along that desert road, for we have missed our objective. And as we drive we remind ourselves that now we are travelling the way he came that evening of 13th May 1935, when, at high speed, he swerved his motor-cycle to avoid two boys on bicycles, went out of control, was thrown over the handlebars and fatally injured. We pass what must have been the very spot, and almost at once see the little National Trust signboard, so unobtrusive beside a high wooden gate and fence that it had escaped us first time; and there, equally self-effacing, as though hiding from our intrusion, is Clouds Hill.

In fact, T. E. Lawrence—or Private Shaw, as he was at the time—had no notion that any habitation lurked there when he was passing one evening in 1923 and paused at the sound of hammering amongst the trees. He investigated, and found to his surprise a small, derelict cottage. A Pioneer sergeant from the camp, named Knowles, was doing the hammering. Having built himself a bungalow in the hollow across the road he was now filling his spare time by leisuredly restoring the near-ruin.

'I covet the idea of being sometimes by myself near a fire,' Lawrence wrote soon afterwards to a friend, telling him that he had taken the cottage 'with the hope of

While serving as a private at the Royal Tank Corps camp near by, T. E. Lawrence found the secluded cottage derelict. He restored it and made Clouds Hill the oasis and only settled home of his remaining years.

having a warm solitary place to hide in sometimes on winter evenings'. He rented it at first, then bought it with money raised from the sale of a gold dagger he had brought from Mecca, and joined Sergeant Knowles in the now purposeful task of making it habitable. Later he was writing from there to another of his many correspondents:

'. . . the cottage is alone in a dip in the moor, very quiet, very lonely, very bare. A mile from camp. Furnished with a bed, a bicycle, three chairs, 100 books, a gramophone of parts, a table. . . . No food, except what a grocer and the camp shops and canteens provide. Milk. Wood fuel for the picking up. I don't sleep here, but come out at 4.30 p.m. till 9 p.m. nearly every evening, and dream, or write or read by the fire, or play Beethoven and Mozart to myself on the box.'

A vision of contentment arises from those words, and at the thought of the contrast between cottage and barrack life. But contentment was not much known to T. E. Lawrence, or Private Shaw, or Aircraftman Ross, or whatever else he called himself, or wherever else he went. For his sanity's sake he needed a degree of privacy, in the same way that he had to try to outstrip thought and frustration by hurling himself about the country at enormous speed on his motor-cycle. Another man of his inclinations might have turned monk, or at least made of Clouds Hill a monkish cell. This could not be Lawrence's way. For reasons which it is hard for ordinary minds to grasp, he had deliberately forsaken the legendary heights he had attained as the hero-figure 'Lawrence of Arabia', in favour of self-abasement in the lowest ranks of the services. 'The man at the bottom sees most,' he told a friend. The Royal Air Force had been his choice. Compelled to leave it because of the publicity he attracted, he joined the Tanks, hated it, but would not toss in his hand and deliver himself up to serve his country in one of the high capacities more appropriate to a war-time leader and Fellow of All Souls. Life at Bovington Camp tormented him: he longed to return to the Air Force, though only on his own terms: he analysed himself remorselessly, found endless fault with his achievements, qualities and character: he threatened suicide.

This was the frame of mind he brought with him to Clouds Hill in the evenings, and assuaged with music and quiet and sometimes conversation with a few intelligent comrades from the camp, or with some distinguished person visiting him. One of the former, Alec Dixon, a Tank Corps corporal then, has pictured a typical evening:

'T.E. was an expert at "mixed grills" where men were concerned. He presided over the company, settling arguments, patiently answering all manner of questions, feeding the gramophone, making tea, stoking the fire and, by some magic of his own, managing without effort to keep everyone in good humour. . . . Some of us used chairs, others the floor, while T.E. always ate standing by the end of the wide oak mantelshelf which had been fitted at a height convenient to him.'

One of the eminent visitors, E. M. Forster, has recalled of that sitting-room:

'It was, and it is, a brownish room—wooden beams and ceiling, leather-covered settee. Here we talked, played Beethoven's symphonies, ate and drank. We drank only water or tea—no alcohol ever entered Clouds Hill. . . . T.E. slept in camp, coming out when he could during the day, as did the rest of the troops.'

Later, when his translation of Homer's *Odyssey* brought him money, he was able to pay for improvements to the place, though he did many of them himself: but it

54

remained essentially the 'one man house', as he described it in a letter to Sir Edward Elgar, telling him of the joy his music had given to the little gatherings in front of the great gramophone horn in the attic-like sitting-room. This is the house as we find it still: still brownish with wood and leather; still book-lined and gramophone dominated; still one man's place, essentially the retreat of a bachelor who would not have cared, as most of us might, to make his private sanctum as different as possible in softness and colour from the barracks hut a mile away, lest the contrast prove too difficult to tolerate. It is compact, but not at all cosy: ascetic, lacking an atmosphere of ease. There is no concession to domesticity: not even the luxury— or burden—of a kitchen. Three glass domes, in what Lawrence termed the Eating Room, used to cover respectively bread, cheese and milk. They are the only acknowledgment of any appetite not emotional or intellectual.

Even sleeping was a haphazard business at Clouds Hill. Lawrence would lie comfortably in his sleeping-bag, marked *Meum*, on the great leather divan in the Book Room downstairs. Another such bag, inscribed *Tuum*, was available for one guest, who would use it on the ship's bunk in the Eating Room. Other visitors were content to lie where they could: on the leather settee of the Music Room, or in the ugly square Book Room chair in which Lawrence liked to sit reading, his book propped against a metal stand of his own design. Also designed by him, and wrought locally, were the three-part fender and the holders for the candles which, with oil lamps, provided the only illumination. There is no electricity connected.

Lawrence's own books are gone, but the shelves are filled with less precious copies of them. The additions to the contents as he knew them have been made with admirable restraint, consisting mostly of photographs, paintings and drawings of him by various eminent hands, and some of his own photographs of the sites of the archaeological work in Asia Minor and Egypt before the First World War which brought him the knowledge of the Arab character that he was soon to turn to such inspired use in engineering and leading the revolt against the Turks. There are also some of the line drawings and pastels by Eric Kennington which illustrated the 1926 subscribers' limited edition of *The Seven Pillars of Wisdom*, to remind us that it was in this retreat that Lawrence did a great part of the work on his masterpiece.

It was typical of him that Bernard Shaw's fulsome praise of *The Seven Pillars* provoked, as well as pleasure, despair. 'There's another ambition gone, for it was always in my hope to write a decent book: and if I've done it there seems little reason to do another.'

'What muck, irredeemable, irremediable, the whole thing is!' he wrote to Edward Garnett on another occasion. 'How on earth can you have once thought it passable? My gloomy view of it deepens each time I have to wade through it. . . . There isn't a scribbler in Fleet Street who wouldn't have got more fire and colour into every paragraph.' This was the note in which he declared '. . . I'm no bloody good on earth. So I'm going to quit. . . .'

The urgent intercessions of Garnett, Shaw, John Buchan and others turned the threat aside, and Lawrence lived on to write further at the simple table desk, lighted by the Music Room skylight. His longed-for return to the Royal Air Force meant leaving Clouds Hill for long periods, but he returned whenever he could and, in 1935, retired there. For a time the cottage became a place of siege, as reporters and photographers persisted in trying to make him talk and pose. He locked himself in, opening the door once, briefly, to reach out and punch a photographer. Only when he ran out of firewood and could no longer stand the din of stones being tossed on to the roof did he come out. It was a distressing incident, which would never have occurred if he had given a brief press conference and stood for a few pictures. His refusal merely served to intensify rumours that he was about to assume some major role connected with the country's defence. As Bernard Shaw had said of him, he had an extraordinary talent for backing into the limelight, that 'limelight of history [which] follows the authentic hero as the theatre limelight follows the *prima ballerina assoluta*'.

Soon, however, the disturbance was over, and Lawrence was left in what should have been peace. He was depressed and unoccupied, unable to think of writing anything more demanding than a few letters, irritated by the ceaseless fluttering of a bird against his window-pane. But he wrote to Lady Astor, on 8th May, that wild mares would not persuade him away from his 'earthly paradise' of Clouds Hill. Besides, he added, there was 'something broken in the works . . . my will, I think'.

Five days later, driving back from sending a telegram to Henry Williamson, agreeing to discuss a proposal that Lawrence might be the one man capable of negotiating successfully with Hitler, he had his fatal accident. What might perhaps have culminated in a return to major service to his country was, ironically, brought to nothing by a cause other than his often repeated refusal to accept any further responsibility in his life. He died six days later. He was forty-six. He is buried not far from Clouds Hill, in the country churchyard of Moreton, in a simple grave that is always covered with flowers.

COLERIDGE COTTAGE

Nether Stowey, Somerset

SAMUEL TAYLOR COLERIDGE 1797–1799

'BEFORE OUR door a clear brook runs of very soft water,' wrote Samuel Taylor Coleridge in 1797, soon after his arrival at the picturesque thatched cottage in Nether Stowey, Somerset, which his friend from university days, Thomas Poole, had found for him in his native village.

Today the stream which runs before the cottage door is strictly vehicular. In high summer the former 'lonely farmhouse between Porlock and Linton, on the Exmoor confines of Somerset and Devonshire' looks balefully on to a never-ending bustle of holiday traffic entering the street of the village which scarcely existed in the 1790's. Not many of the motor-cars bring visitors to the cottage: it is still remote in terms of deliberate pilgrimage, and there is nowhere much for the chance passer-by to pause and park before the flood bears him on. Also the cottage is a good deal changed externally and internally from what it was; and only one room—the original kitchen, now transformed into a small parlour-museum—is open to the public. All the same, 'Coleridge Cottage' is worth a visit, if only because the trouble has been taken to preserve it at all, a gesture, surely, which in this destructive age deserves encouragement. The literary interest of the place lies not in the exhibits it houses, but in the memory of its association with the composition of some epoch-making and still widely familiar poetry.

Coleridge, with his wife Sara, his infant son, the fated Hartley Coleridge, Nanny, their servant, and Charles Lloyd, a Birmingham banker's son who had attached himself as paying guest out of veneration for the poet, began their tenancy near to Christmas, and, despite the season, Coleridge was soon writing in a letter: 'Our house is better than we expected. There is a comfortable bedroom and sitting room for C. Lloyd and another room for us, a room for Nanny, a kitchen and outhouse. Before our door a clear brook runs of very soft water. We have a very pretty garden, large enough to find us vegetables and employment; and I am already an expert gardener, both my hands can exhibit a *callum* as testimonials of their industry.'

Not many months later he 'was fortunate enough to acquire an invaluable addition in the society and neighbourhood of one to whom I looked up with equal reverence whether I regarded him as a poet, a philosopher, or a man'.

This paragon was William Wordsworth, who, with his sister Dorothy, had settled at Alfoxden. They were not to stay many months in the neighbourhood; but poetry would have been notably the worse had they never come at all: for it was during a walk together in the Quantock Hills that Coleridge and Wordsworth conceived the idea of composing together that robust and universally admired ballad *The Rime of the Ancient Mariner*.

Neither the Wordsworths nor the Coleridges had much money, and the original notion was to compose something which would bring them a certain five pounds from the *New Monthly Magazine*. It was Coleridge who suggested basing a ballad on a dream recounted to him by a friend. Wordsworth, who had only just been reading a volume of seafaring reminiscences, put forward the idea of attributing the mariner's misfortunes to his having killed an albatross in the South Seas, 'and that the tutelary spirits of these regions take upon them to avenge the crime'.

They began to compose that same evening, but it was soon obvious that their respective styles of approach were not going to match. The truth seems to have been that while Wordsworth was doing his workmanlike best to contribute a share of the lines, Coleridge was in the grip of an inspiration of a kind that had never visited him before. Though he had scaled some heights already, he had suddenly, without expecting it, come upon the peak which he was to occupy so briefly before the long descent.

So Wordsworth withdrew, and we know *The Ancient Mariner* as Coleridge's. But their collaboration was not at an end. As Coleridge wrote down line after line of his narrative—it embodies, incidentally, a number of direct references to places in the Nether Stowey neighbourhood—it became obvious that the finished product, both in quality and sheer quantity, was going to be worth much more than the aimed-for five pounds. Then the two poets hit on a scheme arising from numerous discussions they had had in recent weeks on 'the two cardinal points of poetry, the power of exciting the sympathy of the reader by a faithful adherence to the truth of nature, and the power of giving the interest of novelty by the modifying colours of the imagination': in other words, poetry natural and supernatural. The thought struck them that it would be interesting to compose a series of poems of both kinds and publish them together in one volume. Wordsworth, who was already moving towards a style of poetry which would catch the fancy of the unintellectual public, undertook to contribute those verses which were 'to give the charm of novelty to things of everyday'. Coleridge would attend to those which would seek to present the imaginary with all the semblance and impact of the real—as he was already doing in the case of *The Ancient Mariner*. So was born the famous *Lyrical Ballads*, its very title revolutionary, whose contents marked a special point in the careers of two major poets.

Also at Nether Stowey Coleridge composed such fine things as *Frost at Midnight*, *Love* and the fragment *Christabel*; and it was there too that he 'wrote'

Then a lonely farmhouse, this was the Nether Stowey home of Samuel Taylor Coleridge for the brief period in which he wrote his most enduring works.

that enduring piece *Kubla Khan*, whose curious origin he described himself, in the third person:

'In consequence of a slight indisposition, an anodyne had been prescribed, from the effects of which he fell asleep in his chair at the moment that he was reading the following sentence, or words of the same substance, in Purchas's *Pilgrimage*: "Here the Khan Kubla commanded a palace to be built, and a stately garden thereunto. And thus ten miles of fertile ground were enclosed by

The parlour-museum was the kitchen in Coleridge's time. A laudanum bottle is on the mantelpiece: in this cottage he had his hallucinatory inspiration for Kubla Khan.

a wall." The Author continued for about three hours in a profound sleep, at least of the external senses, during which time he has the most vivid confidence that he could not have composed less than from two to three hundred lines; if that indeed can be called composition in which all the images rose up before him as things, with a parallel production of the corresponding expressions, without any sensation or consciousness of effect. On awaking he appeared to himself to have a distinct recollection of the whole, and, taking his pen, ink, and paper, instantly and eagerly wrote down the lines that are here preserved. At this moment he was unfortunately called out by a person on business from Porlock, and detained by him above an hour, and on his return to his room found, to his no small surprise and mortification, that though he still retained some vague and dim recollection of the general purport of the vision, yet, with the exception of some eight or ten scattered lines and images, all the rest had passed away like the images on the surface of a stream into which a stone has been cast, but, alas! without the after restoration of the latter.'

It is not certain whether Coleridge had in 1797 begun to turn to the opium which was soon to dominate his life and take away his poetic gift, so this may or may not have been an opium dream. Nor is it known who was this person from Porlock, or what his business, though many amusing speculations have been made. Could he have been a representative of the local chapter of the Secret Service, come to ask a few pointed questions about the inflammatory talk which had given rise to local suspicions that Coleridge, the Wordsworths and certain of their Radical visitors were somehow connected with spying for Buonaparte? At least, one might argue, the 'person's' visit must have been of some importance, since the inspired poet did not ask him to go away and return in an hour, or to sit quietly with the newspaper in another room, while he dashed off the rest of *Kubla Khan*.

No doubt the answer is much more prosaic. But it cannot be said that Coleridge's time at Nether Stowey was lacking in events, whose memory makes a visit to their scene worth while.

SHAKESPEARE'S STRATFORD-ON-AVON

WILLIAM SHAKESPEARE 1564–1616

THERE is no reference to Stratford-on-Avon in Shakespeare's plays. Strong hints appear here and there: the Forest of Arden; the entertainment of Christopher Sly by Marian Hacket, the fat ale-wife of Wincot or Wilmcote, the home of the poet's mother. An anonymous play of the 1590's contains a character called Philip Sparrow, who declares, 'I'faith, sir, I was born in England at Stratford-upon-Avon in Warwickshire', and goes on to add that he has a fine finical name. This is probably a veiled gibe at the young man from the country whose dramatic hits and high patronage aroused the splenetic envy of less successful playwrights.

The Shakespeare Identity Guessing Game has been played fervently and continuously throughout the last century and a half, with some astonishing suggestions for candidature and a firm majority vote that 'the Lad of all Lads was a Warwickshire Lad', his life neither better nor worse documented than that of his contemporaries. Indeed, far more remains of him than might be expected. He was highly sensitive to the ravages of Time and the demolition gang. 'When I have seen by Time's fell hand defaced The rich proud cost of outworn buried age; When sometime lofty towers I see down-raz'd, And brass eternal slave to mortal rage . . .' One fell hand or another has taken his London dwellings, his theatres, everything in the capital that was his; yet has mercifully spared four whole houses in his native town that he knew well and two outside it. The house he chose and lived in, New Place, was destroyed by an irascible eighteenth-century tenant, but his garden remains a garden still.

Stratford, a quiet market town when her astonishing son was born there in 1564, is a hub of tourism and culture today, somewhat overlaid with sophistication and the tedious commerce of the souvenir shop, its small streets choked with cars and coaches. Some rather nasty modern buildings have replaced decent old ones. Ancient inns, once 'simpler than the infancy of Love', have turned their attention to the provision of steaks and scampi. Yet the town has stubbornly retained her country air and a sort of rustic innocence. Catch her on a spring morning before the crowds have arrived, when there is dew on the grass of the water-meadows, and the scent of alyssum in the small bright gardens on Waterside is distilled honey, and you will see the essential Stratford, whom time cannot wither nor custom change to her lovers.

Although much impenetrable mystery surrounds Shakespeare, factual and circumstantial evidence leaves little or no doubt that this was the house in Henley Street, Stratford-on-Avon, in which the greatest of all writers was born in 1564.

All that remains of the house where Shakespeare died in 1616 are the foundations, the well and the gardens. An eighteenth-century clergyman, irritated by tourists, demolished it.

Across the old bridge from the south, across the swan-crowded Avon, the traveller sees for the first time the mellowed pink of the Memorial Theatre, crowned with the yellow flag that bears the falcon crest of the Shakespeares. The gentle slope of Bridge Street brings him in a few minutes to Henley Street, and the most famous of the Shakespeare properties: the birthplace.

Here John Shakespeare, bearer of arms, master-glover, landowner and alderman, was living when his third child, William, was born. The house was then two separate buildings, the 'West House' being the dwelling-place of the family, the 'East House' John's shop or warehouse. It remained in the hands of Shakespeares or Harts, descendants of Shakespeare's sister Joan, until the eighteenth century, suffered various vicissitudes, including the conversion of the East House to an inn, the Swan and Maidenhead, and then became a much exploited place of pilgrimage. That enthusiastic American Washington Irving was pained, on his visit in 1815, to find charlatanry and fakes, such as those objects made from the bard's mulberry tree 'which seems to have as extraordinary powers of self-multiplication as the wood of the true Cross'.

Since those days the responsible stewardship of the Shakespeare Birthplace Trust has made the house deserving of its countless visitors. Outside, it is a homely, substantial, half-timbered structure of Warwickshire stone and wood; inside, an Elizabethan home, comely and cheerful. Like the other Shakespeare properties, it has been handsomely furnished with Elizabethan and Jacobean articles. In the living-room, which would have been the general parlour, John would have sat by the hearth of an evening on just such a good carven chair, clay pipe in hand, Mary at the other side in her best branched gown, their growing family about them. Later this room may have heard William's announcement to his parents that he would have to marry Anne Hathaway of Shottery, and shortly too. To this house he must have brought her after marriage, to live with the old folk, as the custom was; and the children, Susanna and the twins Hamnet and Judith, were probably born here in the traditional birthroom, a bright, airy apartment of white plaster and solid timbers.

When the house was being restored in 1950, such small intimate relics were found as a wrought-iron brooch-pin of the sixteenth century, fragments of glass the Shakespeares may have looked through, old pipes, wine bottles and coins. Such mute witnesses as these, together with documents telling the story of the house and its inhabitants, rare books and manuscripts, are in the museum which is in what was once the East House. Upstairs is the only piece of furniture with a Shakespeare tradition, a desk from Stratford Grammar School, which legend says was Shakespeare's—leant on, written on, wept on by the sleepy, inky, much-beaten small boy who suffered from the Welsh pedagogue Jenkins and later pilloried him in a play as Sir Hugh Evans.

Outside the house has bloomed for a century a Shakespeare garden, full of

Perdita's flowers and Ophelia's, quince and medlar, willow and rose. Walk from Henley Street to the corner of Chapel Lane, and you find a garden that he knew: the Great Garden of his house, New Place, and the trim lawns that contain the foundations of the house itself, the family's drinking well, an intricate, fragrant Knott Garden such as Elizabethans delighted in, and a mulberry tree descended from one that he planted.

> *Of mighty Shakespeare's birth the room we see;*
> *That where he died in vain to find we try,*
> *Useless the search, for all immortal he,*
> *And those who are immortal never die.*

Unfortunately for Washington Irving's noble sentiment, the reason why we cannot find the room where Shakespeare died is that the Reverend Francis Gastrell tore it down along with the rest of New Place, in the middle of the eighteenth century, infuriated by the curiosity of tourists. It was not quite the New Place Shakespeare knew, having been partly rebuilt in 1702, but much must have remained of the house that was to Shakespeare what Gad's Hill Place was to Dickens, a fine residence, early coveted, won at last with patience, economy and toil.

He had left Stratford and his father's home in the mid 1580's, some say to follow the Players to London. From 1585 to 1592 are the 'lost years'. So far as is known, he had become a playwright in London, suffered at the hands of the fair cruel maid who was his unknown Dark Lady, had travelled through the dark night of the soul in this and other ways. His only son had died at the age of eleven. There may have been estrangement between himself and Anne, for there are such sinister pointers in the plays as that reference to 'the dark house and the detested wife'. But all the time he was saving money, avoiding the dissipations to which other theatre folk gave way: becoming a 'warm man'. He had kept up his connections with Stratford, where, tradition says, he returned once a year. In 1597 he bought New Place, paying £120 for it. Though still in and of the theatre, with a lodging in London, this was his home where he could enjoy the company of his growing daughters; where, looking out on to his garden, his flowers and fruit trees, dove-house and barns, he wrote his latest, most mature plays. Daughter-figures, Perdita and Miranda, appear in them. Jealousy and passion were past; the wise, weary Prospero retired to his study and indulged in a little gentle bargaining and litigation. Documents from this time, some of them bearing the crabbed signature with its arbitrary spellings, belong to the Birthplace Trust. On some appear the names of his neighbours—Thomas Quiney, the brothers Combe, Hamnet Sadler, who may have been godfather to his son, and Thomas Nash, the man who was to marry Susanna's daughter, Elizabeth.

The Nashes lived next door to New Place, in the house which now contains the New Place Museum of Local History. Its half-timbered front, replacing a Georgian one, gives a fair idea of how Shakespeare's dwelling looked. It is full of fine things, and has yet another of the lovely gardens which are so much part and parcel of the Shakespeare houses. Shakespeare must have known it well, as he did another house, Hall's Croft, a few minutes' walk away in Old Town. It belonged to Dr John Hall, who married Susanna in 1607. He was only twelve years younger than his father-in-law and seems to have been a favourite with him, as was Susanna herself: 'witty above her sexe', compassionate and cheerful, says her epitaph. Preserved in Hall's Croft are Dr John's medical notebooks, with their fascinating details of contemporary ailments, including those of his family and himself, but not, unfortunately, of Shakespeare. Part of Hall's Croft is used as a Festival Club.

The reality of Anne Hathaway's Cottage, a mile from Stratford, at Shottery, far surpasses those countless cliché reproductions on tea-cosy and ash-tray. It was Hewlands Farm in Shakespeare's day, and the woman he courted an 'old maid' of twenty-six. He was eighteen. The story of that courtship and of the events that led up to the mysterious and furtive marriage is all 'a blank, my lord'. They probably sat on just such an upright, uncomfortable courting settle as stands now in the house, watched sharply by Anne's stepmother Joan, and inquisitively by her three small half-brothers. Then, away from prying eyes, they wandered out into the orchard behind the farm, or across the fields to Luddington, in the peaceful early evening with Venus high in the sky above the apple boughs; and then Susanna was on the way, and the Worcester Diocese was being besought for a special licence for the couple to marry before, in every sense, Advent.

A few miles from Shottery is Wilmcote, and the home of Shakespeare's mother, the well-connected Mary Arden. It is the house of a well-to-do yeoman farmer of Tudor days, picturesque, sturdy and handsome. Not only the dwelling-house but the outbuildings have been preserved, and contain a collection of Warwickshire bygones: agricultural implements, bowls, churns and pails from the dairy, wheelwrights' tools, firearms, lanterns and stocks, all objects once handled by the rough palms of Dick the Shepherd, Robin Ostler, Greasy Joan, log-bearing Tom and their companion rustics. Asbye's Farm, as it then was, came to Mary Arden by her father's will, and young Shakespeare must often have visited it.

The outlying Shakespeare villages are all unspoiled and quietly charming, and the blossomy Vale of Evesham lies beyond them, a refuge on days when too many visitors overwhelm Stratford. On such days the seeker after peace and the purist may well complain. But Shakespeare, a good business man if ever there was one, would smile approval on any commercial enterprise that brought prosperity to his townsfolk. He would smile less warmly on the deterioration of train services that has taken place in recent years, making Stratford accessible from London only by the expenditure of infinite time and patience: a ludicrous situation for Britain's chief tourist centre. A case of 'Gallop apace, you fiery-footed steeds'.

DOVE COTTAGE

Grasmere, Westmorland

WILLIAM and DOROTHY WORDSWORTH 1799–1808
THOMAS DE QUINCEY 1808–1834

IN MAY 1799 William Wordsworth and his sister Dorothy decided it was time they settled down in a home of their own. Northerners born and bred (William's birthplace was Cockermouth, Cumberland, and he had gone to school at Hawkshead, between Windermere and Coniston), the brother and sister had for some years led a wandering life. The serious, idealistic young man and the delicately perceptive young woman, both raptly absorbed in the beauties of natural scenery and objects, were perfect companions each to the other. For a time they had been separated, when William's republican sympathies had taken him to France at the beginning of the revolution:

'*And his heart was all*
Given to the people; and his love was theirs.'

The development of the Terror, however, had appalled and disillusioned him, and a love-affair with the patriotic Annette Vallon had left him emotionally un-settled. He returned, chastened, to Dorothy and lyric poetry. A year and a half at Alfoxden, in Somerset, during which they were near neighbours of Coleridge, produced the *Lyrical Ballads*, so many of which dealt with Lake District scenes and characters. Then, after a short tour of Germany and an interlude at Sockburn-on-Tees, William and Dorothy set up house at Dove Cottage, hard by the lake of Grasmere.

It had once been an inn, The Dove and Olive-Bough: a name boding peace and contentment to the 'simple water-drinking Bard'. Dorothy was housekeeper and cook, William gardener and handyman. He wrote his poems and she her Grasmere *Journal*, which gives a detailed and intimate account of their life and is unrivalled among diaries for its frankness and sensitivity: Dorothy too had a poet's soul.

The cottage, as we see it today, is in essentials as it was at this happy time. It is small, unpretentious, white-painted; a typical Lakeland cottage surrounded by a sturdy stone wall. A room that was once a kitchen, later a parlour, leads into a pretty, part-panelled room that was first Dorothy's bedroom, then William's. It is cool, flag-floored, and contains an elegant wash-stand and toilet set that have come from the Wordsworths' next home, Rydal Mount. Among the portraits may be the very one which the young Keats identified when he dropped in at Rydal years later and found the elder poet from home: 'I was much disappointed. I wrote a note for him and stuck it over what I knew must be Miss Wordsworth's portrait.' On the staircase stands the cuckoo clock whose voice cheered and soothed the ageing poet, long after he had left Dove Cottage, through nights of insomnia and nightmare.

> *The mimic notes, striking upon his ear*
> *In sleep, and intermingling with his dream,*
> *Could from sad regions send him to a dear*
> *Delightful land of verdure, shower and gleam,*
> *To mock the wandering Voice beside some haunted stream.*

Wordsworth announced in a sonnet that he was not one

> *who much or oft delight*
> *To season my fireside with personal talk*
> *Of friends, who live within an easy walk,*
> *Or neighbours, daily, weekly, in my sight.*

Yet, with the friendliness of the north, these dropped in to visit, and were entertained to tea in the upstairs sitting-room where the poet also worked on the new edition of the *Lyrical Ballads*, or sat meditating 'in the loved presence of my cottage-fire'. Now the room contains Wordsworthian furniture and pictures. Then perhaps a poem finished and dictated to Dorothy, or the great Preface to the Ballads concluded (it has been described as the most original single document in the whole history of English criticism), he would go downstairs and engage in the healthy exercise of making the little stone stairway which still traverses the garden, or set off with Dorothy for one of their delightful walks:

> *My sister! 'tis a wish of mine,*
> *Now that our morning meal is done,*
> *Make haste, your morning task resign;*
> *Come forth and feel the sun.*

Sometimes William's sailor brother, John, accompanied them. One day in 1800 William and John set off on a visit. Dorothy's *Journal* records her feelings: 'My heart was so full that I could hardly speak to W. when I gave him a farewell kiss. I sate a long time upon a stone at the margin of the lake, and after a flood of tears my heart was easier.'

Her grief was comprehensible. She, who had been all to William, was to be supplanted in his love by another woman, Mary Hutchinson, who had been at school with William and had later become a friend of both. She was beautiful, kind, sensible, with an extraordinary gift of silence which must have been one of her chief charms.

Formerly an inn, Dove Cottage was the Lakeland home of William and Dorothy Wordsworth for seven years, and their opium-eating friend Thomas de Quincey's for the following twenty-six.

For some years, it seemed, she had haunted William's fancy. As long before as 1794 he had issued a romantic invitation to her to dwell with him in 'Grasmere's quiet Vale':

> *Yes, Mary, to some lowly door*
> *In that delicious spot obscure*
> *Our happy feet shall tend.*

On 4th October 1802 they were married. Dorothy was almost frozen with sorrow. She did not go with William to church. Sara Hutchinson, Mary's sister, 'dear little

70

Sara', prepared the wedding breakfast. The wedded couple returned, and Dorothy flew 'faster than my strength could carry me, till I met my beloved William, and fell upon his bosom'.

She had accepted the position, and they all settled down at Dove Cottage together. There was an element of melancholia in the situation, content as were William and Mary, and anxious as was William to show his sister that he loved her no less. Nearly all the short poems written before his marriage are concerned with her, written to celebrate their joy in Nature and his indebtedness to the 'dearest maiden' who had shown him in her 'gentleness of heart' the pleasures of leaf and flower, young lamb and green linnet. Then, Dorothy's wounded heart forgotten, he surged into his 'grand' period of poetry: *Intimations of Immortality, Resolution and Independence, Ode to Duty* and *The Prelude*. This Wordsworth's voice is 'of the deep; it learns the storm-cloud's thund'rous melody'. Too many poems of other periods were uttered with that other voice 'of an old half-witted sheep which bleats articulate monotony'.

In 1803 Mary, his early 'phantom of delight', had become 'a spirit, yet a woman too . . . the reason firm, the temperate will, endurance, foresight, strength and skill'. She was now the mother of baby John, and in the next year of a daughter, Dora; in 1806 another boy, Thomas, arrived. The little house was getting smaller; Dorothy moved into the 'outjutting' room. Coleridge came to stay often, and long.

> *Great wonder to our gentle tribe it was*
> *Whenever from our valley he withdrew;*
> *For happier soul no living creature has*
> *Than he had, being here the long day through.*

There was another visitor to take up room.

> *A noticeable man with large grey eyes,*
> *And a pale face that seemed undoubtedly*
> *As if a blooming face it ought to be,*

wrote the poet, in one of his ovine lapses. It was Thomas de Quincey, philosopher, opium eater, dreamer and most delightful of men. He loved the Wordsworth women and children on sight, and they him. Of the poet he was just a little afraid. The austere, silent person of ascetic habit, tall, hawk-nosed and unsmiling, was a strange friend for the cherubic lover of life and woman. But friendship there was, and when the Wordsworths left Dove Cottage in 1808 De Quincey took it on a seven years' lease: he stayed there twenty-six years.

He was so delighted with his new home that he could not find time to write to his mother. For neighbours he had the Wordsworths, and the inevitable guest Coleridge; and near by at Elleray the stalwart John Wilson, dominant force of *Blackwood's Magazine* and later famous as 'Christopher North'. Walking, eating great Lakeland

71

teas, sailing on Windermere, entertaining friends: here were many of the 'constituents of happiness' he had drawn up on his first visit to Dove Cottage, lacking only No. 11, the education of a child. Even this was supplied. In 1814 he was introduced to the Simpson family from The Nab, an old farmhouse at the foot of Nab Scar. The daughter, Margaret, a beautiful, stately blonde, the 'beloved M——' of the *Confessions of an English Opium Eater*, bore him a child in November 1816. Money troubles had stood in the way of their marriage, and there had been some local cold-shouldering of Margaret, which Wordsworth, who was held in such respect, might have prevented by championing and protecting her. But the poet may well have thought De Quincey's playful affectionate manner towards Dorothy to have been a sign of matrimonial intentions. If so, he doubtless resented his friend's association with another woman, and one below him in station. A rift opened between the two families which was never quite healed.

In February 1817 De Quincey and his Peggy were at last married, and he brought her and the baby home to Dove Cottage. Here, in their first idyllic years together, he was a happy man. 'Candles at four o'clock, warm hearth-rugs, tea, a fair tea-maker, shutters closed, curtains flowing in ample draperies on the floor, whilst the wind and the rain are raging audibly without.' In 1817 opium entered his life again, in spite of Peggy's influence, and with it came pain, nightmare and the necessity to write for money. More children were born. Dove Cottage filled up with them and with their father's multitudinous books. In 1821 they were obliged to leave it and move to a larger one farther down the lake, the *Confessions* already written and published. In 1834 De Quincey finally, reluctantly, gave up the tenancy of Dove Cottage.

It is a quiet place, among mountains with clouds resting upon them, and by the calm lake; its singular air of peace not only, one fancies, the child of its situation, but of the long, contemplative hours spent in it by two remarkable literary men whose home it was.

HILL TOP

Sawrey, Lancashire

BEATRIX POTTER 1905–1943

'MY BROTHER and I were born in London; but our descent, our interest and our joy were all in the North Country.'

The writer is Beatrix Potter, an essential countrywoman who came into the world on 28th July 1866, in a terraced house in North Kensington. The north was in her blood, however, for Grandmother Potter had been Miss Jessie Crompton, of a family of violent individualists and eccentrics. 'Generations of Lancashire yeomen and weavers, obstinate, hard-headed, matter-of-fact folk,' Beatrix called them. Writing late in life, and with farming experience behind her, she said that she was a believer in breed: in the ability of a strongly marked personality to influence its descendants for centuries, just as a good bull, stallion or ram can become the ancestor of many champions.

It was a simile whose indelicacy would have horrified Beatrix's mother, and the cool, passionless society of Kensington. The small Beatrix was kept isolated as far as possible from the crudities of everyday life, a meek lonely child in a grim nursery, playing with three dolls and a flannelette pig. Behind the grave childish face and the smooth hair were a keen faculty for observation, a poetic imagination and an ardent love of Nature, shared by her younger brother Bertram. They were fortunate in that the parent Potters frequently left home on long visits to country houses, for Rupert Potter was a moneyed gentleman of leisure. There was Camfield Place, near Hertford; Chorley Hall, Grandmamma Potter's home; Wray Castle, on the shores of Windermere; and Dalguise House in Scotland. Around them Beatrix and Bertram roved, collecting plants and animals alive or dead; if dead, skinning and dissecting them for experimental work. The results they drew and painted, Beatrix with a phenomenal skill for her age. The living animals had names: a mouse called Hunca Munca, a hedgehog called Mrs Tiggy-Winkle.

Bertram escaped, in early manhood, from the claustrophobic life of Bolton Gardens, and became a farmer in Scotland. It was not given to Beatrix to join him or to strike out independently for herself. Like the dutiful Victorian daughter she was, she had to accompany Mamma and Papa everywhere, obedient to their every whim. Her mind—a strong, virile, Crompton mind—was unfolding, expressing itself in her secret journals. For her own pleasure she drew and painted exquisite little studies from nature. She began to design Christmas cards. Her parents thought this a daring thing to do, and did not encourage it greatly. When it came to Beatrix becoming at first friendly with and then engaged to such a vulgar tradesman as a publisher, they were horrified and forbade the marriage. For once Beatrix gently defied them. But early and sudden death took Norman Warne away, and left Beatrix once more prisoner to a coldly demanding Mamma and an ailing, restless Papa. She had met Norman because his firm had published some tiny books she had written and illustrated—*The Tale of Peter Rabbit*, *Squirrel Nutkin*, *Mrs Tiggy-Winkle* and others—based on her own childhood pets and later animal friends, and set in delicate glimmering landscapes, idealizations of the Lakeland country she loved to visit. The family spent more and more time in the north. It did not shock or surprise the elder Potters when Beatrix, with a small legacy from an aunt and the *Peter Rabbit* royalties, bought Hill Top Farm, in the village of Sawrey that lies between Windermere and Coniston. It was to be an investment; a respectable sort of thing for a maiden lady no longer very young. There was no question of Beatrix making it her home, although she was now thirty-nine.

But from the moment she saw it it was the home of her heart: a little old farmhouse with an untidy pink rose straggling across its face, a flag floor in the kitchen, dark beamed ceilings and stout doors. Its windows looked down a winding path and over Esthwaite Water to Coniston Fells, a land which she was to make peculiarly her own.

She began to install herself in Hill Top, to implant her personality on it, improve and renovate it: the presence of Mr Samuel Whiskers and his brother rats had done much to harm the old fabric. She installed a 'hind', John Cannon, to look after the place while she was being dragged round England in the wake of her parents. What joy she had in exploring her 'investment'! A wall four feet thick, with a staircase inside it: she had never seen 'such a place for hide and seek'. Cannon was buying ewes—there would be lambs in spring. Young pigs were growing, Beatrix was planting cottage flowers in the garden, the gifts of neighbouring villagers. She was beginning to look like a villager herself, in her wooden pattens to keep out rain and mud, her thick skirts and the shawl over her head. Sometimes it was a sack, not even a shawl. There was little Kensingtonian about Miss Potter now, and if her parents noticed the change spreading into her life with them, we do not know their reactions.

In the eight years after she bought Hill Top she wrote thirteen books for children, six of which are set in Sawrey and particularly at Hill Top. The rooms, scenes and details which appear in the jewel-like small pictures are still to be seen there. The attic of the Roly-Poly Pudding; Mrs Tabitha Twitchit's grandfather clock; the wall where Tom Kitten and his sisters so naughtily climbed, the road down which the three Puddle-ducks stalked wearing the Twitchit family's cast-off attire; the dresser of *The Tale of Samuel Whiskers;* the farm on which Jemima Puddle-duck lived and made her seriously bad mistake about the foxy-whiskered gentleman: all the scenes

In her Lakeland farmhouse of Hill Top, Sawrey, Beatrix Potter found independence from domineering parents and the inspirations and setting for her animal stories and paintings.

of these books are to be found in and around Hill Top. You can see in a doll's house the actual plaster food that Tom Thumb and Hunca Munca found so unpalatable, and the French dolls that belonged to Beatrix herself. The china, the homely furniture, are all arranged as she specified in her will. She had described Hill Top as 'a funny house that would amuse children'; but it had become to her the epitome of all she had ever wanted. Her love, her diligent restoration, and above all her immensely strong personality, imposed a character upon the house as marked as that belonging to a place which has been the home of one family for many generations.

Yet it was never truly a home to her, in the sense of being a permanent dwelling-place. Captive still to convention and her parents, she could only snatch a week now and then to live at Hill Top. The cosy Lakeland cottage one sees today is a creation, the child of Beatrix's fancy. Its rooms are the magically cosy interiors of her paintings. It is not a place in which one feels that real people have been born, have lived and died (though no doubt many of them did, long before Miss Potter set foot in it), for it belongs to the birds and animals of her books, who have truck with neither birth nor death: only with their own immortality.

In 1909 she bought nearby Castle Farm. The purchase introduced her to a local solicitor, William Heelis. A friendship sprang up, and four years later they were engaged. At Bolton Gardens there were parental storms, painful scenes. But at last Beatrix got her way, and in October 1913 married 'Willie', the kindly man who was to be the perfect husband for her.

Now that she was Mrs Heelis, Beatrix Potter was briskly buried. The bustling Lakeland farmer had no time for her *alter ego*. What remained of that phantom (for had Beatrix Potter ever been quite real?) dwelt at Hill Top, kept as a house of happy memories, a retreat from too much company and a place to write in occasionally. A few books were published after her marriage, mostly built from material already collected. They lack the radiant quality of the earlier work. Now real animals took up her time: she became an expert on Herdwick sheep, and bred pigs who were less fortunate than Pigling Bland. She also bought land instead of painting it. Long before, Canon Rawnsley, a founder of the National Trust, had fired her with his own enthusiasm for preserving natural beauties, and she fulfilled his ideals as he could not have dared to hope. When she died in 1943 she left as her lasting memorial six thousand acres of Lakeland country, bequeathed to the National Trust; and among her bequests was Hill Top Farm.

'Tom Kitten's House' is a delight to children, and to all those who were once children and treasured those small tales and their characters. It seems strangely unconnected with Mrs Heelis, that formidable, tough farmer who does not even seem to have liked children very much. The lady of this house, one feels, is shy young Miss Potter, the sleeping princess of Kensington, who had the unusual happiness of seeing the dream of her life realized in every particular.

HAWORTH PARSONAGE

Yorkshire

THE BRONTË SISTERS 1820–1855

The house is old, the trees are bare,
And moonless bends the misty dome;
But what on earth is half so dear,
So longed for as the hearth of home?

The mute bird sitting on the stone,
The dank moss dripping from the wall,
The garden-walk with weeds o'ergrown,
I love them—how I love them all!

THE DANK MOSS still flourishes; the mute bird has been supplanted by the endlessly complaining rook; if the garden-walk is now trim, it is besieged on two sides by the weeds and tangle of soaking grass amongst the graves of children and short-lived adults. Haworth is an inhospitable-looking place even today: what it was like when Emily Brontë wrote her poem one can only shudder to imagine.

Yet she loved it, passionately. It was bleak, remote, pitilessly harsh: a killing place. The family had come from Hartshead, near Dewsbury, with some notion that the air of the hill top between Bradford and the empty moors would cure the invalid Mrs Brontë. It did not. She died, the first of almost all her family to do so there, murmuring: 'Oh, God, my poor children—oh, God, my poor children!'

Five small girls and one small boy were left to the somewhat inept handling of their father and a formidable aunt. The small Georgian house of Yorkshire sandstone, 'with not a tree to screen it from the cutting wind', was as cheerless as its surroundings. Charlotte Brontë's girlhood friend, Ellen Nussey, visiting the house in 1833, noted that there were no curtains to the windows and 'not much carpet anywhere.' The Reverend Brontë had a pathological horror of fire, largely as a result of having conducted so many child funerals after fires started by candles. Combustible furnishings were kept to a minimum.

There is a general absence of carpeting and drapes still, as part of the attempt that has been made to show the house as it was then. Yet there is an insistent air of

Gravestones in the churchyard of Haworth half surround the unlovely hill-top house where all but one of the Brontë family lived and died, and where two of fiction's most passionate masterpieces came astonishingly to be written.

cheerfulness about it, as if in delight that the grim days are no more. The rooms are brighter than one can imagine them having been: the added foyer and exhibition rooms make a healthy modern contrast, even if they have been criticized as anachronistic: the staff who attend to the hundreds of thousands of visitors are mostly, and appropriately, lively, handsome young women. But from the windows the unchanged scene catches the eye: empty moorland or gravestones.

Not long after their mother's death the four eldest Brontë girls were sent away to the Clergy Daughters' School at Cowan Bridge, near Kirkby Lonsdale. Insanitary conditions and harsh discipline were too much for them. Maria, aged eleven, was sent back to Haworth to die of consumption, followed by Elizabeth, aged ten, who died the month after 'of a low fever'. Charlotte and Emily survived, though the horror of their experiences never left them. For Emily the exile produced an almost manic attachment to the dismal parsonage which caused her intense suffering whenever she was forced to leave it again.

Back at Haworth the nine-year-old Charlotte became 'mother' to her younger sisters and brother. Their life was not unhappy, and for some years they were able to enjoy their companionship in peace. They came of mixed Irish and Cornish stock, a fertile mixture for imagination. While their father kept to himself in the small parlour off the hall, where his spectacles, pipe, tobacco box and matches lie today on the table beside the open Bible, giving a strong feeling of his presence to the room, they would gather round the fire in the kitchen behind the chilly dining-room, in the company of the family servant, Tabitha Aykroyd. While Emily baked bread and Charlotte ironed, Branwell and Anne listened with them to Tabitha's Yorkshire tales. Unhappily we cannot quite picture this cosy scene, for not much of the kitchen remains. Like some other parts of the house it was much altered by a later owner, and attempts to reconstruct it and furnish it with some of Tabitha's original utensils have only partly recaptured its character.

One day Mr Brontë brought home from Leeds a box of wooden soldiers for Branwell. From games with these the children built up a daydream kingdom, Glasstown, which developed into a whole fantasy life based on the imaginary country of Angria and the island of Gondal. All four of them wrote endlessly about the elaborate history and lore of these mythical territories; millions of words in all, as often as not in microscopic writing in little manuscript books as tiny as two inches long. 'We had very early cherished the dream of one day becoming authors,' Charlotte was to write in womanhood. Some of these miniature works are on show at the house, and perhaps the most poignant feature of the whole place is the tiny upstairs 'children's study', as they knew it, where they conducted the affairs of their imaginary domains and scratched drawings, still to be seen, in the plaster of its walls.

In their teens Charlotte and her sisters were sent away to be governesses. Left to himself, Branwell, the bright hope of the family, set up as a portrait painter in Bradford. But the dark influences were at work on him: he returned home in debt, took to heavy drinking and opium. The Black Bull in Haworth's steep, narrow main street became his second home. The visitor can still take a reflective drink there in 'Branwell's room'. Its sad modern *décor* has at least left the bell-pull intact, for one to imagine the insistent jangle as the unhappy Branwell summons yet another brandy.

In the Parsonage he and his father shared a bedroom. Both died in it. Branwell had another room for a small studio, which now contains some of his paintings. He had little training and no overwhelming talent for his art; but he painted portraits of his sisters which give an uncanny impression of what one feels must have been their true character.

In 1848, his white hope long since gone, he died of the consumption which was to claim them all. Three months later Emily followed him, refusing medical treatment to the last and dying on the sofa which is still in place in the dining-room. Anne died next year at Scarborough, where she had gone in vain to improve her health.

Only some three years had passed since Charlotte, Emily and Anne had produced their first work to be published, *Poems by Currer, Ellis and Acton Bell*. In the same year each sister had written a novel: Anne, *Agnes Grey*; Emily, *Wuthering Heights*; Charlotte, *Jane Eyre*. Incredibly out of three works produced simultaneously in this moorland isolation by spinster sisters of limited education and experience, two would gain places on the uttermost heights of English prose.

By 1849 Charlotte and her father were left alone. His sight was failing badly. Now famous, she stayed to care for him devotedly, making the house more comfortable and cheerful with furnishings bought out of her earnings. When she was thirty-six she received a proposal of marriage from her father's curate, Arthur Bell Nicholls. She seems not to have cared much for him, but he gradually won her affections. Her father opposed the marriage stubbornly, upsetting her cruelly; but, in his way, he was all too right. After a year of married happiness Charlotte died, her inherent consumption complicated by pregnancy. We can stand in the room in which she died, and where her mother had died so few years before, and look from the windows across that acre of graves. Near by are the two fir trees planted by Charlotte on her wedding day. She knew more happiness in that room than she can have anticipated from marriage.

The church beyond the graves is not that in which Mr Brontë preached. Eighteen years after his death—he was the only sturdy one, living to the age of eighty-four—the old church was demolished and the present one built. A Brontë Memorial Chapel was dedicated in 1964. Two pillars stand at its entrance: at the foot of one the entire family, except Anne, lie in their vault.

In 1876, four years too late to persuade Mr Brontë's successor not to alter the house, the Brontë Society was formed at a meeting in Bradford Town Hall. A small Brontë museum was opened above a bank in Haworth two years later. A long-lived native of Haworth, Sir James Roberts, who had actually spoken with Charlotte, bought the Parsonage in 1928 and gave it to the Society for a museum. Mrs Helen Safford Bonnell, of Philadelphia, entrusted to the Society her late husband's notable Brontë collection; and so the Parsonage became the rightful centre of Brontë scholarship and interest.

There are no Brontë descendants. Haworth Parsonage and its contents are all that are tangible of the once large household. To visit that Spartan refuge on a wuthering height, to imagine beyond the imposed cheerfulness back to the starkness of it in the 1840's, and then to be free to leave, is to come closer to the essence of the passionate masterpieces it saw conceived.

80

Charlotte Brontë's portrait gazes down into one of the rooms she made more cheerful out of her royalties from Jane Eyre. *She and her father were the family's only survivors, and her days too were numbered.*

HUGHENDEN MANOR

Buckinghamshire

BENJAMIN DISRAELI 1848–1881

SUMMER RAIN was falling on the gardens of Hughenden Manor when we arrived there. The primroses, Disraeli's own flower, were over; roses had taken their place. Pied wagtails pecked about on the lawn before the house, as their ancestors had done when the carriage swept round the drive, bringing Dizzy and his Mary Anne back from London to 'those beechen groves of Bucks which even Julius Caesar could not penetrate'.

The beechen groves of the Hughenden Valley are almost as rural as they were in 1848, when the manor became Disraeli's property. Only a mile and a half away is busy High Wycombe, its proximity seeming improbable. One reaches Hughenden by way of twisting country lanes. From its lodge-gate a path crosses a cattle-grid and winds up a hill, past little Hughenden church, to where the manor nestles in its park.

Its façade, a sort of neo-Jacobean, staidly pleasant, is not that of the original Hughenden. A house stood there in Norman times, the property of Odo, Bishop of Bayeux, later that of the Catholic Dormer family, of the Fourth Earl of Chesterfield of *Letters* fame and many others. What the Disraelis bought for £35,000 was a simple, countrified structure, eighteenth century in character, far from perfect to Victorian eyes. But the situation, the air, the beauty of the landscape, were irresistible to Benjamin Disraeli. He loved Buckinghamshire, knew it well (his father had bought a Tudor house at Bradenham in 1829) and, in 1847, with three important novels behind him and a dazzling career before him, he decided that it was time he became a country squire. Hughenden's 750 acres seemed the ideal estate for a man of ambition and large ideas. He had not quite enough money for the purchase; in fact, he had none at all. His father put up £10,000, and his friends the Bentinck brothers supplied the balance of £25,000. The large sum did not perturb him. He was potential leader of the Conservative Party in the House of Commons; it was suitable that he should be a landed proprietor, and besides, Mary Anne was very rich in her own right.

We see Hughenden today transformed by Mary Anne's money, in 1862–3. Disraeli's romantic fancy thought it 'restored to what it was before the Civil Wars in which cavaliers might roam and saunter with their ladye-loves'; but in fact it was remodelled

82

Benjamin Disraeli bought his country home, Hughenden Manor, in 1849 when he was novelist, aspiring country squire and would-be Prime Minister. He was penniless and had to borrow all the money.

by the architect E. P. Lamb into a pleasingly restrained essay in Victorian Gothic. Within the arches of the outer hall stand three statues: one of Disraeli when Earl of Beaconsfield, one of the Earl of Derby who was twice his Foreign Secretary, and one of a handsome but plebeian red lion. It was an old personal friend. When, as a fiery, flashy young man of twenty-eight, he had contested the seat of High Wycombe as a radical, he had addressed the townspeople in ringing tones and for an hour and a half from the portico of the Red Lion Inn. His romantic black ringlets streaming, his long, expressive actor's face, his gaudy clothes, his eloquence, were alike dazzling. 'When the poll is declared I shall be *there*'—pointing to the head of the red lion that strode above the portico—'and my opponent will be *there*,' indicating its tail. Exactly the reverse happened, but young Dizzy was undaunted. Two years later, asked at dinner by Lord Melbourne what he wanted to be, he replied calmly: 'I want to be Prime Minister.' Melbourne was sceptical and scathing. But of the new master of Hughenden, in 1848, he was forced to admit: 'By God! the fellow will do it yet.'

Disraeli called the hall within and its staircase his 'Gallery of Friendship'. In it hangs a portrait of the dashing Count D'Orsay, a friend to Disraeli and a lifelong influence on him, to whom he dedicated his early novel, the love-story *Henrietta Temple*. Another portrait, of George Smythe, later Seventh Viscount Strangford, shows the original of Coningsby, the hero of the first novel in Disraeli's political trilogy.

An unusual exhibit is the side of a coach. The Disraelis were driving one day to Westminster, where an important debate was to take place. When the coach door was opened, Mary Anne's finger was trapped in it. With superb bravery and self-control, she neither fainted, screamed nor cried, but laughed and chattered as usual, so that her Dizzy might not be upset and have his mind taken off the debate. It was typical of their relationship, and he kept the coach side.

The library of Hughenden was, in Disraeli's day, the drawing-room, and the present drawing-room the library. The roles of the two rooms were transposed by Major Coningsby Disraeli, who lived at Hughenden after his uncle's death. 'My collection is limited to Theology, the Classics and History,' Disraeli had said; but the works of Swift and Molière, and a *History of Agriculture in England*, share the shelves with the Hebrew and Chaldee Lexicon. Among the volumes are many with a royal inscription. Queen Victoria was gratified to hear him say 'We authors, Ma'am'. Her sole contribution to literature consisted of *Leaves from the Journal of Our Life in the Highlands*.

On the desk lies a luxury edition of *Faust*; on its richly embroidered cover the initial 'B' and the Beaconsfield crest. All over the house, and on unlikely objects, this appears; a touching little personal identification of the man who had begun life as a politically underprivileged Jew whose grandfather had come to England as an importer of Leghorn straw hats. There is pathos, as well as pride and power, in the face of the forty-eight year old Disraeli in Grant's portrait over the mantelpiece. The long dark Eastern eyes, the sensual mouth, the high, white brow with its tumble of dark ringlets, all give an impression of melancholy beauty, without the foppish-ness of Maclise's sketch of 'The Author of *Vivian Grey*' or the oriental suavity of *Punch*'s cartoons.

Even in the library is a touch of Mary Anne: her pretty foot, in marble. In the drawing-room she is omnipresent. It is a gay room, all gold and blue, approached through delicate Gothic arches, full of colour and detail. Flowers riot decorously on chair cover and footstool and in the enamelled medallions of the elaborate gilded chiffonier. Disraeli's love of bright ornament, Mary Anne's eagerness to please him and surround him with comfort, are everywhere visible. Her small, charming face, between heavy clusters of brown curls, looks gravely down at the room. She was not a girl when the ambitious young Benjamin Disraeli decided that the widow Mrs Mary Anne Wyndham Lewis would be a highly suitable bride for him. He was thirty-three, she forty-five, but rich. The man who had said, 'I may commit many

84

Disraeli's 'workshop',
where he did much of
his writing, was this
small, homely room.
Queen Victoria came
to spend a contemp-
lative hour in it after
his death.

follies in life, but I never intend to marry for "love",' fell head over heels in love with Mary Anne. Their marriage was one of mutual devotion, of constant tender love and kindness, and 'unbroken happiness'. When she died, aged eighty, Disraeli replied calmly to Gladstone's advice to seek heavenly consolation: 'Marriage is the greatest earthly happiness, when founded on complete sympathy.'

Would Mary Anne, who on her deathbed had found strength to be mildly jealous of Queen Victoria's attentions to Dizzy, approve of the sharing of her drawing-room with the portraits of the two beautiful sisters, Lady Chesterfield and Lady Bradford? After her death he found great comfort in their friendship, and his affectionate heart turned towards lovely Selina Bradford. But she had a husband and family, and Dizzy was about to become Prime Minister. He proposed instead to the widowed Lady Chesterfield. She refused him, and Selina cooled off noticeably. In his last novel,

85

Endymion (named after that classic shepherd who had also loved a Selina), some of his feelings about this last bid for happiness are expressed. He had come to wish everything at the bottom of the Red Sea along with the Suez Canal shares.

Yet another woman dominates Hughenden's dining-room. Victoria, Elizabeth to his Leicester, gave him her portrait, painted after Von Angeli. It shows her elderly, cross, and apparently suffering from a severe cold, but she greatly admired it, and the great courtier whom she had created Earl of Beaconsfield no doubt said exactly the right things about it.

His 'workshop', as he termed it, is a simple, cheerful upstairs room, much as he left it. At its small table he wrote several of his works, including the unfinished last novel *Coningsby*, with its nostalgic beginning. 'Of all the pretty suburbs that still adorn our metropolis there are few that exceed in charm Clapham Common. . . .' A cluster of brown withered objects in a glass case are the corpses of primroses sent by Victoria for his funeral. She came to sit for an hour in this room after his death, and mourned him as she had mourned nobody but her husband. She had wanted to visit him as he lay dying; but Dizzy, quipping to the last, refused because 'she would only want me to take a message to Albert'.

Between 1852, four years after his purchase of Hughenden, and 1881, the year of his death, he was three times Chancellor of the Exchequer, twice Prime Minister, carried the great democratic Reform Bill of 1867, and reached the zenith of his fame with the Berlin Congress in 1878. It left little time for the writing of novels, which in earlier days had been both his political weapons and expressions of the non-political side of his nature: romantic, exotic, florid productions, extravagant as Bulwer Lytton's, yet full of an epigrammatic wit that anticipated the best of Wilde:

> 'My idea of an agreeable person is a person who agrees with me.'
> 'I have always thought that every woman should marry, and no man.'
> 'Sensible men are all of the same religion.'—'And pray what is that?'—
> 'Sensible men never tell.'

'I always intended to die in London,' he said. 'It gives one six months more of life, and the doctor can come to see one twice a day.' He did die there, but by his request his body was brought back to Hughenden, and buried with Mary Anne's in the little church where he had worshipped, on the slope of the hill below his gates, amid the funeral pomps and elegiac rhapsodies he would have thoroughly enjoyed.

> *Victoria's servant takes his rest*
> *Well-earned, and on his faithful breast*
> *Victoria's primrose wreath.*

He, of all returning spirits, would be most happy to see his home preserved as it was, his may trees and beech groves still unfelled.

'Some find a home in their country,' he had said. 'I find a country in my home.'

MILTON'S COTTAGE

Chalfont St Giles, Buckinghamshire

JOHN MILTON 1665

O N 7th July 1665 Samuel Pepys wrote in his Diary: 'The hottest day that ever I felt in my life . . . Lord! to see how the Plague spreads.' And he noted: 'I find all the town almost going into the country.'

It was on the hottest day of a summer over three centuries later that we 'went into the country' in the steps of one who had fled from the Plague in that terrible year. John Milton, poet and Parliamentarian, once Latin secretary to Cromwell, had fallen upon bad times. With the Restoration of Charles II in 1660 his occupation was gone, his political ideals destroyed, his name offensive at Court. Two of his anti-Royalist books had been burnt by the public hangman, and Milton himself was in danger. Under a less tolerant monarch than Charles he might well have lost his head, or met a worse fate—also at the hands of the public hangman; but he was fortunate, and remained undisturbed in hiding.

He was blind. 'His adversaries imputed his blindness as a judgement upon him for his answering the King's book (*Eikon Basilike*),' said a contemporary. The truth was that he inherited poor sight from his mother, and it had been continuously strained by close work over the years. Now it was gone altogether.

> *When I consider how my light is spent*
> *Ere half my days, in this dark world and wide,*
> *And that one talent, which is death to hide*
> *Lodged with me useless. . . .*

At the time of the Plague he and his family were living in Artillery Walk, Bunhill Fields, a place then on the outskirts of London and reasonably airy; but unfortunately for the Miltons it became the site of one of the largest plague pits, to which death-carts brought daily their loads of bodies. It may well have been the almost unbearable proximity of this mass grave which drove Milton to seek refuge in the country. It happened that the Quaker Thomas Ellwood, a friend and former pupil, was living with another Quaker family at Chalfont Grange, in Buckinghamshire. Milton applied to him and, says Ellwood, 'I took a pretty Box for him in Giles Chalfont, a mile

Blind and out of favour, John Milton came to live in his 'pretty Box' at Chalfont St Giles in 1665, when driven from London by the Plague.

from me, of which I gave him notice, and intended to have waited on him, and seen him well settled in it, but was prevented by . . . imprisonment.'

The 'pretty Box' is the only house occupied by Milton to survive today. All his City homes were swept away by fire and time; but the small neat cottage at Chalfont St Giles has been preserved by the Milton's Cottage Trust. In 1887, the year of Queen Victoria's Jubilee, it was decided to raise a fund for it in honour of Victoria and of one of her country's greatest poets; there was also, legend says, a threat that it might be taken to America and reconstructed there, brick by brick.

It has grown in beauty since Milton's day. A print of the early nineteenth century shows it starkly set at the end of the village, its front door and diamond-paned windows looking on to bare ground on which pigs root. Now its ancient rose-covered bricks are clothed with a luxuriant vine, and before it is a large, fragrant, cottage garden, a place of flowers, shady arbours, hidden lawns, and trees that gave a welcome shade the day we visited it. Was it here that he wrote, in the person of displaced Satan, that pathetic reference to the flowers he would never see again?

> *. . . With the year*
> *Seasons return, but not to me returns*
> *Day, or the sweet approach of even or morn,*
> *Or sight of vernal bloom, or summer's rose . . .*

For here, dictating to his daughter, he completed the epic *Paradise Lost*, which he had begun in 1642 and had put aside for political activities. Thomas Ellwood, released from an Aylesbury prison, called on his friend 'to welcome him into the country'.

'After some common discourse had passed between us, he called for a manuscript of his; which being brought he delivered to me, bidding me take it home with me, and read it at my leisure; and when I had done so return it to him with my judgment thereupon.

'When I came home and had set myself to read it, I found it was that excellent poem which he entitled *Paradise Lost*.'

Ellwood again called on Milton, to return and praise the book, adding in his frank Quaker manner: 'Thou hast said much here of Paradise Lost, but what hast thou to say of Paradise Found?'

Milton did not reply, 'but sat some time in a muse'. When he had returned to London, and Ellwood visited him there, he produced another manuscript for his friend's approval, and 'in a pleasant tone' said: 'This is owing to you for you put it into my head by the question you put to me at Chalfont, which before I had not thought of.'

It was *Paradise Regained*. So the conclusion of one great poem, and the entirety of another, were inspired in the peace and seclusion of the cottage at Chalfont St Giles.

We do not know for certain in which room Milton dictated; but there is evidence to indicate that it was in the room to the right of the front door, now known as Milton's study. This room was larger in his time, for a hall-way has been made since. It is low-ceilinged, small and shadowy. His face looks out from print, bust and painting; young, smooth and serious in early years, embittered, ravaged by pain and trouble as he grew older. In the small library this room contains are all his works, including rare first editions of *Paradise Lost* and *Paradise Regained*, and the writings of many of his Puritan and Quaker contemporaries. The most personal relic is one with a mysterious history: it is a lock of Milton's hair.

There are three contradictory stories of its origin. The one usually accepted is that during repairs to St Giles's, Cripplegate, in the late eighteenth century, a coffin identified as Milton's was discovered and opened. The rector, before the remains were reinterred, cut off a lock of hair and preserved it. This seems a fairly likely story. Milton had been dead over a hundred years, but hair is more durable than flesh, and his was long and plentiful. (In the reign of George IV the coffin of Charles I was opened and locks of hair removed.) This frail, wispy tendril is greyish-blond— 'he had light brown hair, his complexion very fair,' says Aubrey. On the wall near by is a copy of that passionate, dazzled outburst by the young Keats, 'Lines on seeing a Lock of Milton's Hair'. It was not this lock Keats saw, but another, preserved in a silver reliquary and now lost.

Across the hall-way from the study is the other room open to visitors, now kept as a village museum. In the great open fireplace many a meal must have been cooked for the Milton family. A giant kettle dominates it, surrounded by spit-rack, ancient frying-pan, bottlejack and a 'hastener' for roasting joints—all the massive para-phernalia of seventeenth-century cooking, among other Buckinghamshire bygones. Paintings and photographs show how little the charming village of 'Giles's' has changed throughout the centuries. Its pond, its church, its green, its one long street, are not very different from what they were in the summer days when Elizabeth Milton and her stepdaughter Deborah did their shopping here, and took back ale from the inn to the man who sat at home in darkness, however bright the sun shone. There would not be much talk, in 1665, of Cromwell's visit to Mr Radcliffe of the Stone House, and of his soldiers' tents pitched in the fields round about. Now, in the little museum, one can see pikes which they left behind, and some of the cannon-balls with which they playfully shattered the church windows. Elizabeth and Deborah were no doubt discreet women, and disclosed little or nothing of Milton's connection with the tyrant Protector over whose death all England had rejoiced.

The Miltons did not stay long at Chalfont St Giles. They returned to London 'when the City was well cleansed and become safely habitable again,' says Ellwood. The modest, pleasant Quaker little knew what a debt English literature would owe to him, both for preserving her poet and inspiring his second great epic. And the cottage, the 'pretty Box', has well deserved its long life and the interest shown in it by visitors from all over the world.

SHAW'S CORNER

Ayot St Lawrence, Hertfordshire

GEORGE BERNARD SHAW 1906–1950

LONG AGO, in an idyllic high summer of pre-war childhood, one of the present writers was dared into approaching George Bernard Shaw in the Malvern Festival Theatre, during an interval of *Too True to be Good*, to ask for his autograph. The request was received with a curt 'No!' Many years later, and this time aptly enough in the cold of late autumn, she suddenly encountered, in a narrow St Albans lane, a tall, upright figure in a 'knicker suit' of grey-green, striding briskly over the cobbles, stick in hand but un-leaned-on, patri-archal beard streaming, an ancient hat of Carlylean distinction on the splendid head. A glance was exchanged: we were the only two living creatures in sight. He passed on. Was it imagination that his step had slowed ever so slightly, that he had looked for—even hoped for—a sign?

In the long interval between these encounters, he had been living at Ayot St Lawrence, Hertfordshire, his home since 1906. His wife preferred London and their flat at Whitehall Court, but G.B.S. spent more and more time at Ayot, the retreat he had chosen because he liked to get away from crowds.

Ayot, by and large, is no more accessible now than it was then. Signs to it from the main road beckon one on, and still one is no nearer. It is always two and a half miles away, until one learns the angle from which to approach and surprise it. The village street is still rurally pretty; nobody has put up the water tower, 'straight and stable, with a colonnade of pillars', which he thought would embellish the village; nor have any other of Shaw's hygienic but unaesthetic plans for Ayot come to pass.

The house itself, named by him Shaw's Corner, stands out among the ancient and lovely dwellings of the village because it is neither ancient nor lovely. It was at one time called the Old Vicarage, but was only built in 1898, a typical villa of the period. Shaw came here in 1906, middle-aged and red-bearded. His striking appearance earned him the sobriquet of 'Old Hair and Teeth' among the village children, who were more impressed by his looks than by his achievements, of which they knew nothing, though he was already world-famous as playwright, political firebrand and sage. At first he kept himself to himself. The First World War undermined his barriers, and the terrible blizzard which swept Hertfordshire in 1915 found him working alongside the village men, sawing up fallen trees which were blocking the roads. There had been fears that this strange man might be a German spy: didn't he keep a light burning at night in an upstairs window? But he allayed such notions by offering his cellar as a shelter in case of air-raids, by giving neighbours of his garden produce, and by other courtesies. Nevertheless they knew to the end of his immensely long life little more of the real Shaw than can be surmised by standing at the wrought-iron gate of Shaw's Corner and gazing at the exterior of the house. To learn more one must go in.

The house has been National Trust property since 1950, the year of Shaw's death. He left no endowment for it, believing that the shillings would roll in as pilgrims flocked to the shrine in their millions. Happily for the Trust, it is a modest-sized shrine and not a mansion. It was his home for forty-four years, and the rooms in which he lived and worked are preserved almost exactly as he left them: so much so, that on coming into the hall one feels that one is visiting him, and that in a moment he will emerge, with a greeting or a 'No!'

The hall is comfortably cluttered. A touch of cosiness is given by one of those fireplaces in which a fire is never lit, but which holds a cheerful stove. The master of the house disliked central heating. In a corner sprouts a hat rack, a tree drooping with recognizable fruit, Shavian headgear that is as much a part of his public image as the beard and the eyebrows. His sticks stand below them, as if warm from his hand.

Surely he expects to return soon, for the piano is open; on its stand a copy of *Messiah* and a book of 'Old English Melodies'. A hall may seem an odd sort of place in which to keep the piano; not, however, if one's wife lies ill upstairs, and likes to hear the music floating up to her, and her husband's strong tuneful voice warbling operatic excerpts and the songs of his native Ireland. The piano is a Bechstein, a singularly plain upright, for the man who had been *The Star*'s music critic, Corno di Bassetto, hated grand pianos. During air-raid alerts in the Second World War he would sit at it, playing as loudly as he could, and roaring out airs from Italian operas. It had its uses; like the cycling machine in the corner for keeping an ageing body fit, slender and tough as whipcord. One can picture the ever-active Shaw leaping from the piano to pedal a brisk few miles before his sparse, vegetarian lunch.

Sunshine streams into the hall from the open doors of three rooms. One sees now that the house's slightly severe exterior is deceptive. It was built when the era of domestic slavery was nearing an end. The stairs are shallow, the rooms a comfortable size, the windows large. It is not pretty or romantic, but eminently sensible and suited to its owner, and must have made an agreeable contrast to the Shaws' old flat in the Adelphi, an Adamesque affair without a bathroom.

Off the hall to the left lies the heart of the house, the study. Here at 10.15 every morning he sat down to write, except on days when the outdoors would call him and he would cross the wide lawns to his little revolving hut in the trees, a study in

George Bernard Shaw took this former rectory at Ayot St Lawrence for peace and quiet in 1906, when he was fifty. He died here after a tree-climbing accident forty-four years later.

miniature, linked to the house by telephone. The desk in the study proper still bears his portable typewriter. He had typed, with two fingers, since typewriters had been invented, for any new mechanical device fascinated him, though he was nothing of a mechanic himself and left it to his secretary to change the ribbons for him. He managed his own files, each carefully if enigmatically labelled: 'Self', 'Touring', 'Languages', 'Keys and Contraptions', 'Novo', 'Russia'. Each cabinet contains something of his astonishing mind, and every object in the room is a clue to its workings.

The bookshelves hold many such clues. *Soviet Communism*, by his friends Sidney and Beatrice Webb, stands close to the collected works of William Morris, whose lovely daughter May Shaw had wanted to marry. Economic difficulties stood in the way, and May settled for a 'mystic betrothal'. The origins of *St Joan* are hinted at in *Historic Portraits, 1400–1600*, and in *The Trial of Jeanne d'Arc*. Many writers have left larger libraries, but few are so indicative of their owner as this one.

Two well-used cameras have come to permanent rest beside the desk. Photography was Shaw's hobby for fifty years, a hobby he loved but never mastered. His doggerel 'Rhyming Picture Guide to Ayot St Lawrence', the last thing he ever wrote, is illustrated by photographs touching in their amateurishness. Bad lighting obscures detail, the tops are cut off buildings, strange angles distort views. There is an utter lack of composition sense, typical of the man who lauded art yet had no ordinary sensual appreciation of beauty, as the ugly furniture of his house testifies.

Charlotte Shaw presides over the drawing-room next door. Over the mantelpiece is her portrait, painted before her marriage, showing a piquant, clever face, her beauty that of the mid twentieth century rather than of her own time. Suffragette, Fabian, playwright, translator, intellectual in her own right, 'the green-ey'd Millionairess' subdued her own talents to her amazing husband's, marrying him in middle age to become his helpmate and companion. Shaw jokingly said that she had married him because he was a genius. Perhaps her nature required greatness to serve. She subdued her own personality so firmly that there is little of it in this room where visitors were received. It is, if anything, the room of someone addicted to serendipity, the snapping-up of trifles—small pieces of china, an unlovely but curiously charming pair of owl effigies: again the obvious absence of sensuousness, a no-nonsense attitude to life.

Similarly the dining-room next door is a cluttered, personal room, its furniture functional, with no pretensions to the aesthetic or the antique. Shaw's ancient 'wireless' set stands by the worn-springed armchair which still bears the mark of his head. He ate at the round table, reading or listening to a news bulletin. He had been converted to vegetarianism by the example of Shelley, and followed it rigidly, affecting to despise the pleasures of eating and looking forward to the time when all should live on air.

When the Archbishop in *Back to Methuselah* says, 'Our English people are the wonder of the world. They always were. And it is just as well; for otherwise their sensuality would become morbid and destroy them. What appals me is that their amusements should amuse them,' he is the mouthpiece of the ascetic Irishman who avowed himself in sympathy with 'the Quaker rule, that doth the human feeling cool'. And yet, paradoxically, this Shaw is also the Shaw who says through Good King Charles: 'It is not that I have too little religion in me for the Church. I have too much.'

Under the large, bright window of the dining-room is a comfortable couch, on whose cushions he used to rest every day; and here, in a November dawn in 1950, he died. Around him were pictures of his native Dublin, documents recording the City freedoms he had been awarded, a portrait by Augustus John, photographs of great figures of the past—Gandhi, Lenin, Ibsen, Granville-Barker. He was happy to die. He had lost Charlotte seven years before. Old age and an accident had trapped him into invalidism, and, like Joan, he preferred death to perpetual imprisonment.

As with Joan, too, death was not his end but his beginning. For a time his fame smouldered, then began to burn again to a steady glow. Of all the lustrous names of his time, his is the one that has become a household word, making an even bigger joke of the epitaph he suggested for himself: 'Here lies George Bernard Shaw. Who the devil was he?'

94

Characteristic Shavian headgear hangs in the hall beside the piano. During air-raids Shaw would play and bellow Italian operatic airs.

KNEBWORTH HOUSE

Hertfordshire

EDWARD BULWER LYTTON 1843–1873

'SOME of you will connect him with prose, others will connect him with poetry. One will connect him with comedy, and another with the romantic passions of the stage, and his assertion of worthy ambition and earnest struggle against

Those twin gaolers of the human heart,
Low birth and iron fortune.

'Again, another's taste will lead him to the contemplation of Rienzi and the streets of Rome; another's to the rebuilt and repeopled streets of Pompeii; another's to the touching history of the fireside where the Caxton family learned how to discipline their natures and tame their wild hopes down.'

The speaker is Charles Dickens; the subject, Sir Edward Bulwer Lytton, the 'Bulwer' whose name recurs over and over again in the letters, diaries and memoirs of the Victorians. Novelist, dramatist, poet, orator, statesman, occultist, patron of the arts—he who became the first Lord Lytton was one of the bright stars of his age, outshining by force of personality as much as by his talents the luminaries around him.

Knebworth's first brick was laid by Sir Robert Lytton about 1500; but Knebworth as we see it is very much what Bulwer made it, continuing the work of his strong-minded mother. Barbara Bulwer-Lytton was a talented amateur artist, but her eye for architecture was sadly at fault. Demolishing most of what had been described as a perfect specimen of Tudor house, she rebuilt it as a Romantic's dream castle, a thing of hectic ornamentation, half eastern, half Gothick, and all delightful to the taste of 1811.

Now time has had its usual softening effect, and the pretentiousness and incongruity have settled down into a kind of beauty. A gentle fertile landscape surrounds Knebworth, its paths lead to an unchanged village, a mile from the Knebworth that grew around the railway station and the Great North Road. The strange towers, domes and pinnacles of the house strike the eye with surprise, as one turns the corner and sees them for the first time.

96

Resembling some 'stately pleasure dome', Sir Edward Bulwer Lytton's Knebworth home is very much what the romantic tastes of his mother and himself made it; but its first brick was laid about 1500.

Only one room remains intact of the old Knebworth. It is the banqueting hall, large, splendid, and still having the oak ceiling, screen and minstrels' gallery of the time of James I, and pine panelling which Inigo Jones may have designed. Above it, at the top of a staircase guarded by negroes and heraldic lions, is the only other room to survive, the State Drawing-room, where Elizabeth I was entertained in 1588. Nothing but memory remains of what it was in Elizabeth's day; redecorated and furnished by Bulwer, it is an ebullient expression of Victorian romanticism, a riot of porcelain, gilding, armorial crest and figurine, the whole dominated by a stained-glass window representing Henry VII, 'to whose blood are akin ye Heirs of Sir Robert de Lytton of Knebworth'. In the fine painting by Maclise of Edward IV inspecting Caxton's press, Bulwer himself appears as a slender knight in silver armour. This is Bulwer the medievalist, as he sees himself. In his library we find him as the world saw him, throughout his life.

The heart of Knebworth is in this room. The walls are covered with Bulwer's books, volumes of reference, history, poetry, fiction, reflecting his wide interests. His desk remains as if the year were 1873, and he had just laid down his pen. In his blotter are notes, scribbles, doodles, sketches, bills, the personal memoranda of a busy author; and the programme of that memorable three-night run of Jonson's comedy *Every Man in his Humour*, in November 1850.

The performances had been given in the banqueting hall in aid of the Guild of Literature and Art founded by Dickens and Bulwer. This grandiose scheme was intended to raise money to improve the lot of struggling men of letters; the money being coaxed from the pockets of rich country folk in exchange for dramatic entertainments given by Dickens and his talented family and friends. John Forster, Douglas Jerrold, John Leech, Mark Lemon, all took part. Dickens's sister-in-law, Georgina Hogarth, played the leading role of Mistress Bridget, and Mrs Lemon stepped in to replace poor Kate Dickens, who, with her usual clumsiness, had sprained her ankle. Dickens himself flashed and shone as the boastful Captain Bobadil. The 'Bulwer Festival' was a tremendous success. 'The nights at Knebworth were triumphant,' Dickens recorded gleefully. Bulwer, a splendid host in oriental robes, brilliant and talkative, enjoyed every minute, particularly the Prologue he had written himself:

> *Hark the frank music of the elder age—*
> *Ben Jonson's giant tread sounds ringing up the stage!...*
> *Each, here, a merit not his own shall find,*
> *And Every Man the Humour to be kind.*

Kindness, however, was not enough. The Guild of Literature and Art proved a damp squib. Bulwer built almshouses at Stevenage, but nobody would live in them. No more plays were given at Knebworth. But during that week of 1850 Georgina Hogarth formed a lifelong friendship with her host, whose personality she found 'magnetic'. His compulsive charm looks out of Knebworth portraits, showing him at all stages of his life. At twenty-eight he is Byronically handsome, a 'talented blue-eyed dandy' of the late Regency, and editor of the *New Monthly Magazine*. (He was seen at the Athenaeum wearing high-heeled boots, a white great-coat, and a flaming blue cravat.) Further on he is the bridegroom of a lovely Irish girl, Rosina Wheeler, for whose sake he has at last defied his dominant mother. They live in London, too extravagantly for what Bulwer can earn by writing; for the angry Barbara had withdrawn her allowance when he married against her wishes.

Another picture shows an older, bearded face, lined with worry. The marriage has ended in nightmare. Rosina, finding herself neglected by her overworked husband, sought admiration elsewhere and turned savagely on Bulwer, badgering and harassing the man she considered responsible for her spoiled life.

But Bulwer was unbeaten. He went on alone, became a successful novelist with his first novels, *Paul Clifford*, *Eugene Aram*, *Pelham*, *The Disowned*, books anticipating Dickens in their element of propaganda for reform of the terrible prison conditions and harsh penal code of the time, and in Bulwer's analytical interest in criminal psychology. Then came the splendid *Last Days of Pompeii*, with its first gleam of mysticism.

At the same time Bulwer was carving out a career in politics, first as Member for St Ives, then for Lincoln: Liberal, but not strongly Whig, and always campaigning on behalf of the victims of 'low birth and iron fortune'. Later he was to change sides, largely owing to the influence of his friend Disraeli, and, as Colonial Secretary, to deliver what Palmerston described to Queen Victoria as the best speech he had ever heard in the House of Commons.

But this was in mid century. In the meantime he had become a dramatist, and at least two of his plays were to endure—*Money* and *The Lady of Lyons*. The year 1838 saw him made a baronet, and in 1866 he was raised to the peerage. In 1843 his mother had died, and he had come to Knebworth, his ancestral home. Here he was to build, write, meditate, and charm his many guests, defying with equal courage unhappy memories, criticism, deafness and the ravages of age.

He fought the years 'tooth and nail', said one who knew him. 'Lord Lytton's hair seemed dyed, and his face looked as if Art had been called in aid to rejuvenate it.' The tall, slim figure became shrunken, the high-bridged nose more prominent, the rich curling hair and beard not quite so luxuriant: yet the man whose personal magnificence had matched that of his home was still striking, still exotic, though decaying as an ancient building decays. In his youthful travels he had met a young gipsy girl, and she had told his fortune:

'You have known sorrows already . . . you will never come to want, you will be much before the world and raise your head high, but I fear you'll not have the honours you count on now. You'll hunger for love all your life, and you will have much of it, but less satisfaction than sorrow.'

It had all come true; it is all there, in a painting over the library mantelpiece.

In his famous ghost story, *The Haunted and the Haunters*, Bulwer wrote a significant passage:

'Such a being . . . loves life, he dreads death; *he wills to live on*. He cannot restore himself to youth, he cannot entirely stay the progress of death . . . but he may arrest for a time so prolonged as to appear incredible, that hardening of the parts which constitutes old age.'

Bulwer Lytton's lifetime fame has faded; he was too much of his age, too mannered, too lacking in Dickensian universality to remain in men's minds by his works alone. He lives on in the portraits, in the vivid word-pictures of his friends, and in the structure of Knebworth. But one flash of prophecy in his late and fine novel, *The Coming Race*, suggests that his star may rise again. For in this ancestor of modern science-fiction he tells a tale of a new race of human beings, each endowed with an equal, unlimited power of destruction, by means of a force called Vril. Sitting at his Gothick window, a chibouk at his lips, a red and gold cloth beneath his hand, he had gazed out at the peaceful Hertfordshire garden and seen—the hydrogen bomb.

INDEX